"*If the Customer's the Copilot, You're* [...] *Seat* provides a practical and actionable guide to help us understand and impact the new 'consumer.' Brian's insight captivates your attention and delivers a timely and inspiring view to build and direct your team. If you're intent on leading and driving exceptional customer experience, you will find the answers and needed insight in Brian's book."

Nancy Splaine, President,
Connecting Point Marketing Group, Inc.

"Brian Dennis has always gone the extra mile for his customers and his teams. His brilliant guidance is cleverly woven throughout the book. This is a must-read for any true customer experience leader's library. Here at Marriott, our 'Spirit to Serve' culture is all about our guests having a great experience. *If the Customer's the Copilot, You're in the Wrong Seat* provides the lessons that help us deliver upon that experience."

Doug Ridge, General Manager,
Gaylord National Resort & Convention Center

"Brian's latest book delivers on the promise its title makes. It's 100% practical and 100% inspirational. Read it. Study it. Steal from it. Most importantly, do something with your teams using the wisdom and stories you'll find inside. At least one of them will become your new north star!"

Mike Wittenstein, Managing Partner, Storyminers

"Brian's book is worth the investment of time. He presents the essence of sustainable customer service in this rapidly changing retail landscape, delivering messages that are easy to understand and apply. At Cisco, we put the Customer First, and Brian really gets it!"

Ron McEvoy, Cisco's Business Transformation Group

"It's been proven that what's on the inside with employees shows up on the outside with customers. Brian provides you with a playbook for increasing customer and associate engagement, and for earning results that come when this engagement is delivered deliberately and with the intention to honor both parties."

Jeanne Bliss, Founder and President of CustomerBliss, and Cofounder of The Customer Experience Professionals Association

"At first I thought this might be just another customer service book. After reading the first chapter, it was clear that *If the Customer's the Copilot, You're in the Wrong Seat* was special. One thing I love about Brian's book is the simplicity in which he writes. Every employee, front-line associate or seasoned manager can benefit instantly by guidance he provides. Don't delay—start reading it now!"

Toni Yacobian, Founder & CEO of The Yacobian Group

"*If the Customer's the Copilot, You're in the Wrong Seat*
is a must-read for Customer Experience professionals
looking to stay ahead of the curve. The winning
combination of engaging storytelling and practical tips
makes Brian's book a pleasure to read. Hats off to Brian for
reminding us, educating us, and inspiring us to block out
the noise, embrace change, and ensure that our customers
are driving our service strategies."

Chad McDaniel, President of Execs In The Know

"Of all the books I have read on the subject of The
Customer, this book by far is the most enjoyable
and eminently practical, as Brian is a great storyteller
with a significant depth of experience. Brian draws from
multiple industries and disciplines using examples—often
humorous—to illustrate and teach us where to look next
for inspiration. If we learn best by example and by doing,
then this is the 'go to' book for your new strategic plan to
improve customer loyalty. Highly recommended!"

*Mary Murcott, President of The Customer
Experience Institute, Dialog Direct, and author of
Driving Peak Sales Performance in Call Centers*

"We believe that happy employees = happy customers =
more profitable business. With his years as a customer
experience innovator, Brian's book will show you yet
another way to create a culture of engaged employees to
make that equation work."

*Jenn Lim, CEO and Chief Happiness Officer,
Delivering Happiness*

"Brian does a masterful job of combining technical facts foundational to customer-centric transformation with practical how-to advice in a compelling and entertaining fashion. His passion about all things customer jumps out on every page and his use of personal stories to drive a point home is brilliant. There is no doubt: this book is a required read for any business leader. Period."

Paula Courtney, President & Chief Executive Officer,
Verde Group

"What I love about Brian's new book is how he makes the connection between employees and customers. Investing in having real people make real decisions with a customer-first lens, and providing the support system and training to essentially create a living culture of customer service—these are real solutions that benefit both the customer and the employee! From dragging Charlie on the golf course to the *Packers Sweep,* his use of stories makes the lessons easy to remember and recall, and creates a fun common language for keeping the lens! Unlike books with catchy slogans and one-hit wonders, this book provides a comprehensive philosophy based in our current customer-centric reality. An easy and delightful read with huge ROI, I highly recommend *If the Customer's the Copilot, You're in the Wrong Seat!*"

Wayne Bennett, President, TeamWorx Team Building

"Brian has been a champion of the customer and retail experience throughout his 20 years with leading retailers. Brian's passion to share this insight and critical piece to retail success comes forth wherever he engages. His extensive retail knowledge and the stories he illustrates in his new book, *If the Customer's the Copilot, You're in the Wrong Seat,* all drive this point home. If you are in any role where the customer is critical to you and your company's success…read this book. You will laugh, find relevance and come away with new ideas on how to better serve your customers."

Daniel Wittner, Chief Operating Officer/
Executive Vice President, RBM Technologies

"Through his use of entertaining stories, Brian Dennis makes strong points that serve as tips, tactics and strategies any business must have to deliver amazing customer service."

Shep Hyken, customer service expert and New York Times
bestselling author of The Amazement Revolution

If the Customer's the Copilot,

You're in the Wrong Seat

Innovative Yet Simple Strategies to Elevate Your Customer's Experience

Brian Dennis

Library of Congress Control Number: 2016910460

ISBN 978-0-9976751-0-8

Editing by Barbara Munson of Munson Communications

Interior page layout by Kerrie Lian, under contract with
    Karen Saunders & Associates

Cover design and illustration by Marty Petersen Artwork &
    Design

Published by ServiceWerkz

ServiceWerkz Press Edition

10 9 8 7 6 5 4 3 2

For orders other than individual consumers, ServiceWerkz grants discounts on purchases of 50 or more copies of single titles for bulk use, special markets, or premium use. For further details, contact:
Brian@BrianDennisSpeaker.com

Dedication

To Frances Dennis, the most wonderful mom and role model a son could ever hope for. Thanks for always being there, for showing me what living integrity looks like on a daily basis, and for inspiring me to share my passion with others.

Table of Contents

Foreword

This is a book about insights—those deep customer needs and behaviors, both known and unknown. It is also about how these insights can be used by companies to engage their customers. Do you want to know how to do this? If you answer yes, read on. If you answer no, you will miss an insightful journey.

Brian does a brilliant job of sharing customer experience insights through storytelling. He demonstrates the storytelling art form by transforming the ordinary into the extraordinary. Imagine that! These real-life stories are not only colored with interesting characters, examples and cases, but they are also supported by facts from the most highly respected research organizations.

In all my years as a customer experience practitioner and university professor, I have come across hundreds, if not thousands, of wonderful papers and research studies on the design and delivery of customer service. I have written and published many of them myself. I have wondered who remembers what I wrote. I know I do not remember most of what others have written. It is not the power of the word that becomes indelible, it is the power of the pictures, images and metaphors that does.

Case in point: Think about the word "thing" and think about the word "garden." What comes to your mind in the case of the first word? I rest my case with the second because I know that it conjures up many varied, vivid and colorful images in your mind. And that is what this book is about— an artist's rendering of powerful ideas that capture the imagination. Brian keeps it simple and memorable.

Few things are as compelling as a good story, and Brian has mastered the art of storytelling. His stories always begin with the end "gem" in mind. He notes, for example, that if you are going to drive your organization to become a customer-focused business, change is inevitable. Everyone says that. But the metaphors and true examples in this book drive home an inescapable, deeply resonant and palpable appreciation of what that means. His stories are accounts of customer experience that create generalizable insights.

If you are like most people, then this is a book that will guide you through a multitude of ideas that are distinctive. It is an anthology of compelling stories revealing gems of wisdom about simple but powerful strategies to make organizations excel at delivering service. Brian's impressive stories and anecdotes drive home points and explain complex ideas. The book will change you, and if it does not, read it again.

Picture yourself (and your pilot) flying through the skies sitting on a magic carpet. How is the view? Feel the coolness of the breeze? The sensation of the height? See the small creatures below? This book is about the sensational view you will gain as you glide through the skies on your carpet.

Put on your lenses, tie your knots and enjoy a journey of ideas as they come to life in every chapter.

Mohamed Latib, Ph.D.
CEO, CX University

Introduction

Since publishing my first book, *Winning at the Front-line: Lessons in Creating the Ultimate Service Environment*, I have had the opportunity to travel all over the country talking to service leaders who are committed, dedicated, and in search of new ways to define their customers. To me, they epitomize what this book is all about: putting the customer in the pilot's seat. Many of these highly successful and accomplished individuals have shared their secrets for redefining the customer and what those secrets mean to their survival.

This book is a culmination of the ingredients that you can use to prepare a service program that really satisfies. It is not formula laden or filled with complex theories. Rather, it is an extension of my customer-service style, personality, and successes. So many of the celebrated stories you will read are the results of others that share the passion for delivering great service. These lessons will help you guide your own path and, more importantly, the paths of others.

You will learn so many wonderful lessons that are relevant, not only to your customer-service applications, but also to so much more. Let me share an example.

An avid professional basketball spectator, I enjoy taking in a game whenever I have the opportunity. Although a die-hard Chicago Bulls fan, I resided in Pennsylvania for a short while and quietly rooted for the home team Philadelphia Seventy-Sixers. The president of the team at the time was Pat Croce, and he knew who the pilot was.

Pat was always on the concourse of the First Union Center greeting people before the games. At one such game, he sees a few guys sweeping the floor. "Hey guys, who's your boss? Rich Habina? OK." So Pat gets on the walkie-talkie and says, "Rich, this is Pat; listen, I have four gentlemen here," and he reads their names off their name tags. "They're off tonight. They're getting paid for their full shift, but they're going to be with me." He takes them down, sits them on the floor, and tells the waitress these four guys are his guests for the night and to let them eat and drink as much as they want, the bill is on him. Before he left them he said, "Thanks, guys."

Now when was the last time you saw a CEO or president greeting workers as they walked into their place of business? How about recognizing the maintenance person in your building and offering them some dinner certificates or a pair of movie tickets? You see, Pat Croce understood that all levels play a part in the success of any business. That is, every aspect from the floor sweeper to the concessionaire are all pieces of the puzzle that form a customer's experience. I can promise you, the next time these four gentlemen go back to work, they will be better at what they do and happier about doing it.

Let's stay with this basketball theme. I now live in Milwaukee, and we were privileged to have a great owner of the Milwaukee Bucks by the name of Herb Kohl. Herb was an amazing businessman, the owner of an NBA franchise (29 years), and a US senator (24 years), but always true to his roots and knew who his internal customers were.

When Herb sold the Milwaukee Bucks, he pledged $100 million toward the construction of a new arena. What most people don't know is, he gave a bonus to every single person in the Bucks organization and to every worker at the BMO Harris Bradley Center where they played.

It was reported that ushers got $2,000 or more and some longtime Bucks employees got enough to pay off their mortgages or to buy new homes. In total, Kohl gave away over $10 million.

"The people who work at the Bradley Center, many of them are minimum-salaried people," Kohl said. "To them, $2,000 was a fortune. I was happy to do it and they were deeply appreciative. It doesn't change my life, but it changes theirs."

One more example and I promise to get off the sports theme. Just prior to publishing this book, I had an opportunity to spend some time with Bill Squires, who is the owner/president of Right Stuff Consulting. Bill is considered the foremost expert on stadium management and has held top-level positions with Yankee Stadium, Giants Stadium (two tours), Cleveland Browns Stadium, and Disney's Wide World of Sports Complex. He currently serves as a liaison between the New York Football Giants team and the New Meadowlands Stadium Company, which operates the $1.7 billion MetLife facility.

What really impressed me about Bill is not just what he said, but rather what I witnessed at MetLife Stadium early in the morning when the employees were arriving. As they entered the facility, seeing Bill standing nearby, many of them walked over to shake his hand. Some even gave him a hug. There was an enormous amount of respect and admiration from the frontline employees. This man who holds a prestigious position within the organization is also the first one to jump in and assist an usher, security, or any other of the hundreds of tasks that are required on game day. These associates knew and respected Bill because he earned their trust through his everyday actions and witnessed not only how he treated the fans/customers but, more importantly, how he interacted with them.

Great external service begins with internal management that inspires and exhibits the traits of a customer-driven organization. We just witnessed that with Pat, Herb, and Bill. Far too often I have examined businesses that fail to orchestrate a successful program internally and later are left scratching their heads at why it doesn't work externally. In order to deliver service that is absolutely customer-driven, your business structure must be fully integrated— at all levels—throughout.

The guiding philosophy of providing great customer service has not changed much over the years. Today we are armed with greater knowledge, more sophisticated customer profiles, better training . . . you get the gist. Even with all that, the objective is fundamentally the same as it was 30 years ago: make sure your customers are happy. Should be simple. Right?

Retail is changing and it's changing fast. In fact, it's predicted that it will change more in the next five years than it has in the last 50. That's partially a result of customer adoption of new communication technologies that continue to compress in time over the last century.

Just look at radio. It took more than 35 years to achieve a consumer adoption rate of 50 percent. Cell phones took only 15 years to reach the same level and, incredibly, social media only 3.5 years. The message for retailers is quite simple: While you literally had decades to perfect your radio-era customer strategy, with the advent of social media you might be lucky enough to get a year, and very soon even a year may be too long.

My life has been dedicated to giving others the tools that will help them achieve happiness in not only their lives but also the lives of others through a customer leadership approach. The contrast between customer leadership and traditional leadership is the difference between treating the customer as the pilot versus the copilot.

There is a story of a man who was walking down the road. He sees a guy moving bricks from one side of the road to the other, and he asks him, "What are you doing?" The guy says, "I'm moving bricks." A little farther down the road, he sees a second guy doing the same thing. "What are you doing?" he asks. "I'm moving bricks," the second guy says. Then he goes a little farther and there is a third guy. "What are you doing?" he asks again. And this time, the answer is, "I'm building a cathedral."

That's what I want people to see—where they fit into the whole. Customer leadership focuses on individuals as they see their role as more than just moving bricks. They have to feel the security and reward of building something that they have a rightful part in. If a call center does not properly take a telephone call or if somebody fails to ship the goods needed for a much-publicized sale, then perhaps we risk the customer's needs not being met. We must understand that if any one of us is missing, we cannot make this work.

Throughout the book, we'll take a look at innovative customer experience companies—companies like Shopkick, which is radically changing the customer experience. Shopkick is a mobile app that sends shoppers rewards when they're at retailers like Crate & Barrel, Publix, and Walgreens and is easier than carrying loyalty cards. No plastic cards, no confusing rules, no extra steps—just walking in with a smartphone earns perks.

As you read this book, you will notice that it takes you on an almost simplistic avenue as it walks you through the steps and rewards of being customer-driven. After all, I owe that style to Sister Mary Murphy, who in Catholic grammar school once scribbled on one of my very long-winded papers, "For heaven's sake, if you have something important to tell me, start at the end."

> **SIMPLER IS BETTER.** Lincoln's Gettysburg Address was only 262 words, 202 of them one-syllable.

I have concluded that if NBC can give you the world news in 30 minutes, Winston Churchill can sum up his WWII battle orders in 34 words, and the Biblical story of creation can be told in 600 words, then I too can benefit from this strategy. As a result, I strive to be a reductionist.

Delivering outstanding customer service in today's very fast-paced environment can be challenging. But today's challenges are similar to the task that Sisyphus faced as he tried to push his enormous rock up the hill. It was strenuous but not complex. Delivering a great service experience is both simple and incredibly challenging. Anyone can bounce a basketball up and down and throw it through a hoop. But not many can play like LeBron James. To become as effective a service leader as James is a basketball player, you will need vision, commitment, and a customer lens on all you do.

The information presented in this book reflects that mission. I want you to nibble on bite-size pieces that you will remember and apply to your own situation. This book presents something I have practiced and encouraged throughout my entire life: the awesome power that comes with delivering an exceptionally consistent customer experience.

And finally, let me say this. I am not a writer. In fact, I am not even very good at writing—never have been and probably never will be. How my editor makes any sense out of the pages I send her still bewilders me.

But what I do do well (see, I'm not a writer) is share my beliefs on how to deliver great customer service. When sharing those beliefs, I almost always surround them with a story or example. That's how I teach and present, and it has successfully served me over the years. In fact, I have had many students, business leaders, and conference attendees come up to me many years later commenting on a story I told and detailing how they applied it to their own situation. This book is filled with simple principles, abundant quotations, anecdotes, and stories on how to build a great customer experience. Nothing that you read here will be earth-shattering and sometimes will seem to skip from one story to another. My goal is for you to find the charm in that, but the real trick is to put these examples into practice. Good reading . . .

1

Mastering Change

"Change before you have to."
Jack Welch

"If you do not change, you can become extinct!"
Spencer Johnson

Late one night a sea captain saw the lights of another ship coming straight at his ship, so he had the signalman send a message to the other ship, "Change your course 10 degrees north."

Back came the response from the other ship, "You change your course 10 south."

This annoyed the captain because it was not an appropriate response, so he signaled back again, "I am the captain of this ship. Change course north."

Back came the response, "I am a seaman first class. Change course south."

Now the captain was infuriated. This was an outrageous insult. He told the signalman to send back one more message to tell them, "I'm a gigantic battleship. Change course north."

And back came the response, "I'm a lighthouse. Change course south."

This tale illustrates the importance of having not only the flexibility to change but, more importantly, the willingness. Whether you are a single-person business or an anchor Fortune 500 company, how you adjust to meet the changing customer will play a large part in determining your future success.

The Greek philosopher Heraclitus taught that nothing is permanent except change. Champion organizations will be adaptive businesses that will incorporate a positive outlook of change and will be even better defined as a result. Unfortunately today most organizational cultures are not positioned this way. They are not structured to handle the rapid pace of changes that are thrust upon them. Their customers are changing and they cannot keep up.

There is a great scene in the movie *Spaceballs* when one of the characters asks, "When will then be now?" Well, the answer is very soon and faster than ever before. The winners will be those businesses that can adapt quickly to a customer-first experience that connects the retailer/seller with the consumer no matter where they are and at the moment they're ready to purchase.

Hit the Ball and Drag Charlie

There is an old golfing joke about an avid golfer named Bill who played golf every day with his best friend Charlie. When Bill came home late one evening from playing golf, his wife asked how his day had gone. Bill responded, "Terrible, Charlie had a heart attack on the 6th tee and dropped dead." His wife was stunned and responded that it must have been awful. Bill agreed and said, "Yes it was. From that hole forward it was hit the ball and drag Charlie."

As I travel to many different countries, I often encounter business leaders that are infected with the "hit the ball and drag Charlie" disease. They are often trying to lead change but nobody else is following them. Many times, there are too many Charlies to drag and the organization is never able to make the necessary transition. That is when their customers go elsewhere, and they are left holding the bag.

The concept of connecting with the customer in this brave new world of the 21st century continues to change at light speed. Decade-old ideas are being challenged as fast as customer needs demand. The days of spoon-fed employees who are told how to service customers is over. Businesses paying people to be strong of body and weak of mind are gone. That is what I call the oil-and-water syndrome, and the two do not mix. Rather, customer-driven organizations are paying people who can think, develop, and learn. In return, associates are given opportunities that benefit not only customers but also themselves.

A large part of my background was in the extremely competitive food/drug retail industry. This arena is one of the most fiercely contested grounds on which stores battle for customer count and sales dollars. Every week, executive meetings are held to find ways to increase customer traffic and strategize new sales opportunities. Billions of dollars are spent on print, digital, and television advertising to bring customers into grocery stores on a daily basis.

Over the years, the food industry has been extremely slow to change. Not long ago, it was a group that was waiting for a cat to bark and it will never happen. This sluggishness allowed stores like Whole Foods, Trader Joes, Wegmans, and Aldi to enter the market. They have barely stayed ahead with respect to the customer's needs today, and in very few instances, did they look ahead to servicing the wants of tomorrow's customer. The consumer is the ultimate driver who has changed and will continue to change this industry dramatically.

Let's look at an example. When I went to the corner deli or food store many years ago, lunch started at noon and ended at 1:00. Now, lunch starts around 10:30 and ends after 2:00. Breakfast is no different. When in town, I will usually go to the gym very early in the morning and am showered and ready for the day by 6:30 am. Ready for the day means ready for some nourishment to get the day started. When I stop to eat, these coffee shops, fast food venues, and bagel locations are already brisk with business.

Customers continually challenge the way we do business. It is basically reflective of a lifestyle that they are leading, with days starting earlier and lasting longer. This shift can be a bonanza for those ahead of the curve, or can spell disaster for businesses too rigid to shift their strategy.

Marriott Hotels International builds the majority of its properties from the ground up. As a result, their projects generally run from two to five years from concept to development. Throughout this time, the architects can change the style of the hotel, or even its name. For example, Fairfield Inn was originally going to be called "Marrottel," but at the last minute, Chairman J.W. Marriott Jr. decided to name the property after the family farm.

Marriott is the largest hotelier on the Fortune 500. They are continually striving to increase sales through innovation—and that involves change. Rather than rest on the laurels of many successful years, they have chosen to embrace the wants of the Marriott customer now and well into the future.

To meet the changing needs of customers and consumers, all organizations will need to continually refine their product or service. Flexibility and versatility—so you can respond quickly and effectively to customers' needs—are only part of the mission statement. Consistency and reliability will prove far more important to your customer base and provide a far more accurate measurement of your success.

Is It Saturday or Sunday?

On a recent Sunday after attending church with my family, we entered the drive-thru of a local fast-food chain to get the kids a treat. They each wanted a cheeseburger and nothing else. On Sundays at this establishment, cheeseburgers are only 49 cents. Such a deal, right?

I ordered the two cheeseburgers into this new fancy drive-thru speaker that helps ensure an accurate order. Now this company has spent billions of dollars installing these devices to solve the biggest complaint they had, which was wrong items being given at the drive-thru, so I was assured my order would be handled correctly. After all, they did have state-of-the-art technology helping them out.

I recited the order then drove up to the pick-up window with a single dollar in my hand when a young man greeted me. He said, "$2.11." Never mind the please. A little confused, I asked him if cheeseburgers were still the special on Sundays. He replied, "Yes they are, but today is Saturday." I suggested that he might be mistaken and today is actually Sunday. He looked back at me with a sincere look and said, "No. Today is Saturday because I don't work on Sundays."

At this point, I began looking around thinking I must be on some hidden camera show. Meanwhile, my wife is in hysterics waiting to see my next move. Needless to say, I calmly pointed out to the associate that my family does not typically get this dressed-up on Saturday and that he may want to ask his manager what day it is. He left, came back a few seconds later, and acknowledged it was in fact Sunday, and he had forgotten that he had switched days with his friend.

Although this story is comical, it emphasizes the importance that changing technology and strategy to meet customer needs is only the start. It is just a plan until it is executed. If the improvements are made to adapt to the changing consumer and the implementation is inconsistent, then you have gained nothing but to further alienate your customer.

It seems that every MBA program does a case study of Motorola Inc., who learned a painful lesson when its slowness to deliver digital telephones allowed Nokia Corp., the Finnish firm, to supplant them as the world's largest cellphone provider at the time. Consumers will not wait for you to change and will seek out other less well-known brands and stores if they can deliver the goods consistently. Motorola was left behind by the market shift to digital that customers demanded, and they are still fighting to recover.

Nowhere is transformation occurring faster than in this industry. The cell phone you know today is transforming rapidly from voice to data communication. It is typically a younger customer who is looking for the newest, coolest, and fastest that is available.

How About Those Millennials?

Speaking of a younger customer, you cannot talk about change without acknowledging the group that is rewriting all the rules. Yep, those darn millennials. If you don't think they're coming fast, be aware that in 2016 they outnumbered baby boomers for the first time ever.

There are about 80 million millennials (born 1980–2000) in the United States alone, and they make up some 25 percent of the US population. Ironically, due to immigration, they're actually a generation that is increasing in size.

They are changing the workplace dramatically—for them it's more about collaboration than command and control. They are breaking down the walls literally and figuratively, as their physical environment reflects with open floor plans and transparency. They communicate on the go—no longer with e-mails but rather with brief communication, such as text and chat. The 9–5 workday does not exist and they demand flexibility. Oh yeah, and they want to be engaged by the work and have fun at the same time.

Now as I talk with my colleagues, there is a healthy tension between the old rules of leadership and this new group. There lies the gap and the challenge of change. With that said, I can personally tell you millennials respect what works, but are always looking for new ways of working, leading, managing that produces better results and a team that is more engaged.

On the purchasing side, *Forbes Magazine* calls 2016 the year of the millennial customer. It's estimated they'll be spending $200 billion annually by 2017 and $10 trillion over their lifetimes as consumers, just in the United States alone. That means 30 percent of retail sales will come solely from this group.

One of the best consumer research studies I have seen to date regarding millennial shopping behavior was done by

Christopher Donnelly and Renato Scaff of Accenture. They conducted research on the shopping behaviors of 6,000 consumers, of which 1,707 were millennials. I think the results will surprise you.

They found remarkable similarities between them and their predecessors, the Baby Boomers (born from 1946 to 1964) and Generation X (1965 to 1979). Here are some of the similarities:

- *More than half (55 percent) of the survey respondents, in all three demographics, said that they seek out "the cheapest return option."*

- *Forty-one percent of all three groups said they practice "showrooming"—examining merchandise at a nearby retail store and then shopping for it online to find the lowest price— more often than they did a year ago.*

- *Thirty-six percent of those surveyed from all three generations said they will go online to buy from a retailer's web site if they want a product when the company's stores are closed.*

- *On average, 89 percent said having access to real-time product availability information would influence their shopping choices in terms of which stores they would frequent.*

Another element of their research was a benchmarking survey involving 60 global retailers that focused on six capabilities and asked 80 questions. The following are the six capabilities that they focused on :

- *Providing a consistent customer experience regardless of channel.*

- *Offering connected shopping that allows customers to move across channels to fulfill a single shopping mission.*

- *Developing integrated merchandising skills, which requires retailers to provide an integrated product assortment and unified pricing across channels.*

- *Putting in place flexible fulfillment and returns procedures that offer customers multiple convenient options.*

- *Enabling personalized interactions through which retailers effectively engage customers to offer dynamic, accessible, and continuous shopping journeys, whether in-store, online, or via a mobile device, whichever consumers desire.*

- *Providing better, faster, and more memorable customer experiences.*

Accenture then matched the consumer and retailer bench-marking surveys on a one-to-one basis to evaluate what is important to customers compared to what retailers are actually delivering.

Unfortunately, their research showed that retailers are currently under-delivering when it comes to the demands of millennials. When Accenture evaluated the retailers to understand how seamlessly they deliver the customer experience, they found that most of them had big holes in their approaches. On the positive side, they did credit most retailers with making headway on providing a consistent cross-channel experience and offering personalized interactions. However, the connected shopping, integrated merchandising, flexible fulfillment options, and the capabilities and enriched services that help make the overall shopping experience better, faster, and more memorable all remain as works in progress.

They further concluded that millennials are not only transforming their own shopping behaviors but those of their parents, who are increasingly mimicking the demands of their children for seamlessness as they climb the digital learning curve. One consequence of this evolution is that the retail environment will certainly change faster than many companies expect in the coming years, and many retailers will find themselves falling further and further behind. That's because delivering products and services in a truly seamless fashion will require companies to make profound changes across their entire organizations—changes that many seem either unprepared or unwilling to make.

It kind of sounds like market speak to say the customer's experience is much better when it's "seamless." But when the service delivered is unified and flawless—inbound, outbound, and everywhere in-between—customers will historically rate satisfaction levels much higher.

Many of my speaking engagements are now involved with the health care industry. They are dramatically reworking their processes to stay ahead of an aging culture and keep pace with a younger "I want service now" group. While giving a seminar at the East Coast Seafood Festival, I was alerted by a colleague about a new service her doctor utilized called PatientSite.

When she wants to look at her X-rays or medical tests, she is able to download them on her home computer. If she has questions for her doctor or nurse, she can e-mail them over a secure link as well as request prescription refills online or even make a doctors appointment. This is a major advance as the physician group as a whole has been typically resistant to adapting to new technology. This is clearly evident from a recent survey of 257 doctors, where the results showed only one-third expressed significant interest in using technology to communicate with patients.

In today's fast-paced business climate, it is interesting to witness this evolutionary change that consumers are inflicting upon all industries. Whether you are banking, shopping, spending leisure time, or buying a home, these industries are retooling their long-term viability by taking off the blinders and seeing these huge opportunities that are being created right in front of their eyes.

When we purchased our home, it was very evident that the real estate and builders markets were quickly conforming to the changing needs of the new-house shopper. They are getting creatively closer to their customers by offering amenities seldom seen in this industry. Let's look at a few examples.

There is a builder in Dallas who gave buyers six months of free milk deliveries with an actual milkman showing up on the doorstep in the morning. Another homebuilder in Houston gave one year's free electricity with every home purchased.

New homebuilders are also courting real estate agents. One builder I know of sponsored an Academy Awards night for real estate agents at one of its premier communities. They showed the ceremony on a big screen and rolled out the carpet for them when they arrived while snapping photos like the paparazzi. Not surprisingly, referrals were up 62 percent after this event. Another builder set up a special room in his development for real estate agents called a TREAS (Treat Real Estate Agents Special) room. Inside there was a computer and a lounge where agents could relax and meet clients. A developer in Atlanta had agents put their business cards in a pot and the lucky one that was selected had their company's name and logo placed on Interstate 75 where over 250,000 cars pass each day.

Change happens at different paces and at different levels. Change in itself does not always need to be significant movements or broad radical maneuvers. In Japan, many follow a formula called the Kaizen philosophy that encourages numerous small changes to existing systems, products, or processes, which results in very frequent and very deliberate changes based on changing customer needs.

Companies will often resist ideas that can threaten their namesake product or brand. Gillette is a great example of a company competing in the viciously competitive business of razor blades. They are continuously looking for ways to improve the shaving experience and have progressed from single blades to multiple blades. They were the first to introduce adjustable, shock absorbing and multibladed razors. Their desire to evolve their success and adjust appropriately always keeps Gillette competitive.

At the same time, you can't change just to change, as that can be the enemy of success. PepsiCo learned this when it started to make rebranding missteps a habit. It unveiled a rebranding of the Tropicana orange juice brand. The new concept was so hated by consumers they scrapped the redesign and went back to the old packaging.

Another of their brands is Gatorade. They just celebrated their 50th year in existence, and it is one of the most recognizable brands in the world. After sales volume slipped, Gatorade began its rebranding efforts. It led the US market in sports drinks when it decided to redesign its label from the recognizable Gatorade name to a big letter "G."

The result? Sales dropped even further. Sales by volume dropped 13 percent but the company decided to continue to push the new Gatorade look. In order to explain all of this to their customers, the company actually had to release a commercial called "Gatorade Has Evolved" so consumers could better understand the rebranding.

Bob Hope, the famous comedian, was a master at tailoring material for his audience. He knew that good jokes played better when they hit his customers right between the eyes and sometimes this required change at unusual times. For instance, while traveling on a military trip doing wartime shows for the service personnel, he was scheduled to land in the Azores, but the pilot warned him that heavy winds might prevent the landing. Bob said to his head comedy writer, "Write some wind jokes."

He did. Unfortunately, it was too dangerous to attempt a landing, so they flew into Spain. Bob came down the aisle again and gave the wind jokes back to his writer and said, "Do some Spain jokes." Even Bob Hope, the master of comedy at the time, understood that a change in his audience/customer required a different set of material —and fast.

This book is about customer service, not change. However, you cannot exist in today's competitive arena without adapting to this new consumer. That would be the equivalent of setting the warning light to go on after you already crashed your plane into a mountain. That is why I felt it important enough to address before we even discuss the traits of a customer-driven organization. People resist change, even change for the better—that's a fact. But don't be deterred by naysayers.

It's important to also acknowledge that people in companies and organizations won't change if they perceive the "need to change" to be an indictment of their past performance. Many will assume that change means leadership is not satisfied with individual or team results. Sometimes that is true, but more often than not, it's important to let employees know that your organization changes to keep up with the marketplace and emerging business challenges.

Employees are not always the only ones to resist change. Sometimes senior executives have a hard time letting go of timeworn strategies that once worked well. Kellogg Company is a great example because they face a struggle today similar to one they faced in the 1990s when America's breakfast habits changed. They thought cereal was always going to be their customer's ideal choice for breakfast. In fact, they did not introduce a new breakfast snack after Pop-Tart pastries in 1964 until 1992 when they introduced Nutri-Grain granola bars.

Even as Kellogg grew their operations in some 30 countries, their model still evolved around cold cereal. It wasn't until new CEO Carlos Gutierrez took over and taught his leadership team that cereal was just one breakfast option and what they ate in Battle Creek, Michigan, every morning was not what others around the world were eating. He persuaded company leaders to "change" their thought model and envision people in Japan eating rice, fish, and miso soup for breakfast, while people in India had Khichri, a blend of lentils, rice, and spices.

Gutierrez changed the company's direction, opened a nutrition research center, bought Keebler, and expanded its product mix. When Gutierrez left Kellogg in 2004 to become US Secretary of Commerce, the cold cereal business in the states accounted for less than 50 percent of its business and had expanded to over 180 countries.

Fast forward to today where continued weak demand for cereals and snacks in the United States is weighing on Kellogg. It has been working to make its products more attractive to consumers who are becoming increasingly conscious of what goes into their food. Kellogg has committed to stop using artificial colors and flavors in its products by the end of 2018 and use only cage-free eggs in the United States by 2025. Time will tell if that change is fast enough as their most recent total net sales posted their eighth decline in nine quarters.

Let me be clear. An organization should always be grounded to their current strategy, communicate it properly, and pivot based on feedback as they stay close to the customer. Although strategy should not change with the most recent customer call or last social post. Former British Prime Minister Harold Wilson once said, "The only human institution which rejects change is the cemetery." The first step in mastering change is recognizing that it exists, and the second is choosing to be a part of it.

2

Be Careful, That's a Customer Standing Next to You

"In the world of Internet Customer Service, it's important to remember your competitor is only one mouse click away."

Doug Warner

"Know what your customers want most and what your company does best. Focus on where those two meet."

Kevin Stirtz

If you are a business, what comes to your mind first when you hear the word "customers"? The ones who are buying your goods and services, of course. Nevertheless, there are other customers who are every bit as important as they are. Identifying your internal customers and learning how to take care of them is critical to your future success. It is important before you embark on any customer-service program that the organization defines what internal customer service means to them. It takes an entire team effort to accomplish this task. Just as an airplane needs landing gear and wings to get you on the ground safely, so too does your business.

Think of your organizational structure as numerous grains of sand by the seashore. Rearranging a few granules does not begin to alter the basic characteristics of the beach, whereas a hurricane can move enough sand to give the coast a remarkably different appearance. In the same way, the countless levels of support within an organization give it a distinguishing ambiance. Altering a few pieces of the customer vision will not in itself be significant. However, if the entire organization shares this customer-first culture, then the climate will be dramatically impacted.

I cannot begin to tell you how many fantastic vision and mission statements I have read over the years. Most are on an expensive imported wooden frame or a brass plaque and can be seen in the lobbies of businesses all over the world. They look good and sound even better. Unfortunately, the mission statement on the wall in too many instances does not match the story being told by the organization. For example, a recent SAP study showed that 80 percent of companies rate customer experience as a top strategic objective. However, when asked how satisfied they are meeting that objective, less than 20 percent believed they were doing a good job. When asked, "What makes up a positive customer experience that results in trust?" their answers could be bucketed into four themes:

- *Reliability*

- *Convenience*

- *Responsiveness*

- *Relevance*

I can usually tell you in just a few minutes after walking into a business if that fancy plaque is truly the culture of the organization or just dead words. From the security guard to the receptionist that greets you—they are all walking billboards that reflect the pulse of that business.

Great External Service Starts Internally

The magical question your business must ask is, "How can we expect our associates to deliver excellent service to our customers if this behavior is not fostered inside the organization?" It is impossible to deliver superior customer service organizationally without strong internal service leading the way. The internal customer is anyone within your own business who is dependent on you for whatever reason. By supporting this internal customer, we allow them to take better care of the external customer. The same principles addressed in this book for external service applies to the inside. Customer service has to be a total organizational effort.

Previous studies have shown that when an external customer becomes dissatisfied and leaves a business, they will typically tell ten other people about their dissatisfaction. Those ten tell others, who tell even more people. In the age of the Internet and social sharing, hundreds if not thousands can now be witness to a poor service experience—and very quickly. In fact, recent research by McKinsey Digital Labs shows that 79 percent of customers trust online reviews as much as personal recommendations.

The process that occurs internally is not any different. In fact, it can prove much more damaging than externally. Just ponder the results if your internal associates become dissatisfied. They are not telling nine people but the hundreds of people they come into contact with each day. Multiply this by a few more and you soon have a disease spreading inside your business that will eventually stretch outside.

In the film *Casablanca*, police captain Renault shuts down Rick's Café, loudly declaring that he is "shocked" to discover gambling on the premises, even as he pockets a wad of winnings from the roulette room. This mirrors those service programs that preach to their customers that they are committed to their needs but fail to provide the proper tools to meet them.

Businesses have many functions including but not limited to sales, operations, marketing, technical support, human resources, finance, customer support, and several more that comprise them. As you can see, the mesh of internal communication and service is far-reaching. Therefore, it is critical that management is committed to keep these groups functioning as one.

One example that stands out is the unprecedented success Southwest Airlines continues to have in leading the industry in customer satisfaction. Southwest pilot Frank Gaines demonstrates why internal relationships play such a large role: "Everyone rows in the same direction, and one area where I immediately noticed it was in the relationship between the pilots and the mechanics. Southwest fosters the idea of 'internal customers,' and the pilots are 'the mechanics' customers. I know this sounds corny, but it really works. The mechanics have a great attitude, do great work, and challenge themselves to get the job done with minimal delay to the aircraft's schedule. Compared to my previous employer, it is utopia, and I feel much of the reason is due to the corporate culture at Southwest," Gaines said.

Customer service is perhaps the biggest differential advantage of prominent companies today and will likely continue through the 21st century. This is how your business will primarily be measured against your competition. Price and quality by themselves do not provide endurable differential advantages. That is why it is so critical to involve all layers of the organization into your service plans. Teamwork is crucial to customer-service achievement and this starts with the internal customers.

A CEO was getting feedback from his housekeeping associates that they were not being given enough time to clean their rooms. So he gathered other senior executives of an industrial cleaning supply company, travelled by bus to a cheap motel, and then used the firm's products to clean very dirty rooms. The challenge was to clean one room every 20 minutes, the normal amount of time allotted to the motel's housekeepers. Through this immersive learning experience, executives got firsthand knowledge of how hardworking people use their cleaning products. They learned that the large 3-gallon bottles of cleaning solution were too difficult to use and gained insight that products needed to have labels with instructions written in the first language of the housekeeping associates. This simple move alone slashed five minutes off the cleaning time.

Many businesses have value statements that speak to the customer being "at the heart of everything we do." But what does that really mean and how do you know if it's working? What does it mean to create a customer-centric organization? Bain & Company released research showing more companies than ever before are claiming to be customer focused. Ninety-five percent of management teams say are customer focused—but therein lies the mismatch. 80 percent of these same companies reported that they a "superior experience" to their customers, only 8 p the customers agreed.

Be Genuine

Many years ago, the story goes, when people travelled in Pullman railway sleeping cars, a passenger found a bedbug in his berth. He wrote a letter to George M. Pullman, president of the company, informing him of this unfortunate fact. By return, he received the following response:

"The company has never heard of such a thing and as a result of your experience, all of the sleeping cars are being pulled off the line and fumigated. The Pullman's Palace Car Company is committed to providing its customers with the highest level of service, and it will spare no expense in meeting that goal. Thank you for writing and if you ever have a similar problem, or any problem, do not hesitate to write me again."

However, enclosed with this letter, by accident, was the passenger's original letter to Pullman. On the bottom of which the president had written a note to his secretary:

"Send the S.O.B the standard bedbug letter!"

Oh my. Not very genuine—huh? Today's customers are digital and savvy. They will have access to more tools and resources and are better equipped to identify whether a business is genuine or not. The times are gone where you can afford to say one thing and do another. Your customer will call you on it—or worse, just leave.

Take Responsibility for It

A rookie left fielder for the old New York Giants couldn't seem to catch anything. Easy pop flies were falling for doubles. Base hits were rolling through the rookies legs all the way to the fence.

At last, the Giants manager decided he'd had enough. He removed the rookie from the game and went on to play left field himself. But the manager did no better. He missed a couple of easy chances too.

When the inning ended and he returned to the dugout, the manager turned to the rookie on the bench and said, "See what you've done. You've got left field so screwed up, nobody can play it."

Don't be like that manager. Take responsibility. Customer centricity starts with the leader. I can't dance, but I don't blame my partner, shoes, or the band. Responsibility isn't to blame. It's leadership and great leadership is powerful especially when applied to your customers.

Headquartered in Milwaukee, the Harley Davidson we know today is a living icon and brand institution. However, in 1981, it was about to go bankrupt. Their motorcycles were becoming poorly made and they lost market share to the Japanese companies. So what did they do? They got customer centric. Instead of leadership selling their vision of building a better bike, they took a more contemporary route of enlisting others in refining and sharing this vision. They knew they could only accomplish their goals if they were able to expand their vision to include each and every employee in the plant. In that same year, they gave every employee on the Harley assembly line a button they could push. That button stopped the line. Every Harley employee had the right and, more importantly, the responsibility to shut down the production of hundreds of motorcycles if they saw anything at all wrong with one of the bikes on the line.

The workers took the personal accountability seriously and began finding each other's mistakes. Heck, they even began finding their own mistakes. Those buttons gave them responsibility and that responsibility delivered better bikes.

It may seem odd or even counterintuitive, but a truly customer-centric business looks first at the employees they have before focusing on their customers. This helps create the key enabler to a complete end-to-end customer experience—that is your corporate culture.

There is an interesting paradox when it comes to business and the customer-centric culture. Most leaders understand the importance of culture and the impact it has on the customer experience, yet most struggle to understand it in simple and practical terms. They are led to believe that policy, development, and process will drive culture alone—well, it doesn't. Peter Drucker, the famous modern business guru, said it best: "Culture eats strategy for breakfast!"

Your Hidden Customers

Robert Half International conducted a survey and found out the top reasons employees leave their jobs to go somewhere else. When key executives, managers, and supervisors were asked what they thought, the most frequent answer was "money." They felt money was the motivator that caused employees to leave. Ironically, when the employees who left were surveyed, the number one reason they left the job to seek work elsewhere was lack of recognition and failure to feel appreciated.

In Thomas Crane's *The Heart of Coaching*, now in its 4th edition, he reflects on a study by Glenn Tobe and Associates that surveyed employees and supervisors to find out what their top motivators were. Take a look at the diagram and notice how different the answers were. Pay particular attention to what the employees felt was important as compared to what their supervisors thought.

Employees wanted

1. *appreciation*

2. *feeling "in" on things*

3. *understanding attitude*

4. *job security*

5. *good wages*

6. *interesting work*

7. *promotion opportunities*

8. *loyalty from management*

Supervisors thought they wanted

1. *good wages*

2. *job security*

3. *promotion opportunities*

4. *good working conditions*

5. *interesting work*

6. *loyalty from management*

7. *tactful discipline*

8. *appreciation*

(Glenn Tobe and Associates Survey)

What I find incredibly interesting, the survey results are eerily similar to another that was taken 40 years earlier and an updated one that is coming out in a new book later this year. Same results over a 70-year span—that is managers and employees have differing perceptions of what is important in the workplace. What is so troubling about this survey is that appreciation is free. It does not cost anything to tell an associate they are valued. Go back and think about the last time somebody complimented you or showed appreciation for your efforts. Didn't that make you feel good? Possibly, it made your day.

Let's put the shoe on the other foot. How did you feel the last time that you praised somebody else? Didn't it make you feel warm and fuzzy inside? You bet it did. Best yet, it was a win/win. You felt sensational giving the adulation and the person on the receiving end felt just as terrific getting it. Happy internal associates provide better internal and external service.

Have you ever heard of the Hawthorne Effect? It's a term in psychology that developed out of a study in Hawthorne, California, many years ago. Industrial psychologists were trying to understand how to motivate workers in a manufacturing plant to higher levels of productivity. One theory they tested was the lighting in the plant. Their theory was that if the workers could see better (more light), they would be more productive. As the light level was increased, sure enough, production went up. However, surprisingly, as the light level was reduced, production went up again! They kept lowering the level of light and production was peaking in a plant that was almost dark. How could this be? The psychologists discovered that humans perform better when they know someone is watching them—that someone cares about what they are doing. This is now called the Hawthorne Effect.

Whether it is the Hawthorne study, the Glenn Tobe and Associates study, or just my personal experience over many years of coaching, appreciation is a key motivator in retaining the best associates.

Jan Carlzon, the former president of Scandinavian Airlines, in his best-selling book, *Moments of Truth*, revolutionized how service-oriented businesses look at the organizational support chart. In a traditional layout, companies operated in a pyramid type structure with the CEO at the top and the frontline employees at the bottom.

Jan turned this pyramid upside down and laid the road map for future service-driven businesses to follow. He was emphatic that he would rather have the lower-level employees serving the higher needs. By doing so, he put the customers at the top and the upper management, including the CEO, at the bottom. Perhaps this may be the best-placed example of internal service. It is a pure comprehension that everybody supports each other in the organization.

Throughout my retail management career, I started each morning looking for ways to make it easier for associates to provide the exceptional service I was looking for. This was my primary role of serving our internal customers. When I was feeling really lucky, I would even ask my associates how well I was doing in providing them the tools to service the customers better.

Let's face it, organizations that provide outstanding service have a significant advantage over their competition. As a result, they acquire and maintain associates much better. Companies that exercise exceptional internal service are at an advantage of attracting and keeping good associates. This will initiate the following domino effect: associates are happier, they stay longer, provide better support, stay closer to the customer, and put the front-liners where they belong—at the top.

P.T. Barnum, the great showman, used to exhibit what he advertised as a "happy family." This family consisted of a lion, a tiger, a wolf, a bear, and a lamb, all in one cage.

"Remarkable," said a visitor to Mr. Barnum. "How long have these animals lived together this way?"

"Eight months," Barnum replied. "But occasionally we have to replace the lamb."

There can be no lambs in a service-driven organization. All levels internally and externally must be pedaling in unison. Even the smallest of weak links will cause the chain to fall off.

3

Peanut Butter & Grape Jelly: Never Underestimate the Value of a Great Partnership

"For every thought we have, for every action we take, we get the original, they—the customer—gets the carbon copy."
                    Michael Ryce, Ph.D

"No sale is really complete until the product is worn out, and the customer is satisfied."
                    L.L. Bean

Dick Vermeil, the head coach who led the St. Louis Rams to a Super Bowl victory, offered this parting advice to all who would care to listen. He said, "What it takes to win will never change. It doesn't matter if it's 1980, 1990, 2000, or even 2010, when you surround yourself with good people, who work hard, who work together, who are unselfish, who care about each other, and are not embarrassed to let you know that they appreciate you, you will succeed."

In sports or business, victory usually goes to those that attract and fully utilize the best available resources. Winning is a partnership and one cannot go it alone. It's true what they say: The whole is greater than the sum of its parts.

Your customer-service program is only as good as the team. You cannot undertake this voyage alone. You will need the help of others and support of the team to reach port. In turn, they will need your help and commitment to allow you to all sail together.

Most companies today are sitting on a figurative goldmine. That goldmine is the talents of their associates—talents that are far too often not fully appreciated. In a study of 1,400 employees, two-thirds stated their employer was operating with less than half the available brainpower. In another study, 40 percent of all Americans indicated that they were bored with their jobs. It wasn't that they felt their role was not important, but rather they felt their talents were not being adequately utilized.

If you want to create a partnership within your organization, then unleash the intellectual assets inside your business. Studs Terkel, the prolific author, once remarked that most employees have jobs too small for their spirit. The results are clear. Associates underperform not because they are lazy or unmotivated, but rather, in most instances, because their employers have not taken the necessary time to properly identify their talents.

Go Get Me a Rock

If I work for you and you essentially say, "Hey, Brian, go get me a rock," and so I go get you a rock and I think I have been successful. Then you ask, "What is this?" and I say, "Well, it's a rock." And you reply, "Yeah, but it's not big enough." Oh, ok, so you wanted a bigger rock, so I go get a bigger rock and bring it back to you and here it is. You say, "But it's not a smooth rock." Oh, you didn't say anything about a smooth rock.

Lesson 1 is to set the proper expectations for our associates in terms of what that customer experience should really look like. The better job we do up front to set that expectation, the easier it will be to reinforce, recognize, and give feedback around the experiences they deliver.

A poor man rings the doorbell at a mansion. To the wealthy man that answers, he says, "I haven't worked in weeks. Do you have any odd jobs for some cash?" The rich man says, "You can paint the porch. Here's some paint. When you're finished, I'll come out and evaluate your work." Twenty minutes later, the poor man knocks on the door again. "I'm finished. Would you like to see how I've done so you can pay me?" The rich man looks at his watch and remarks, "That sure was fast. I thought it would take you much longer to paint the porch." To which the man replies, "First, I am pretty good with a paintbrush. Second, you don't have a porch, you have a BMW."

Lesson 2 is you can't just "delegate" your service message without clear direction. Your team needs to see, live, and breathe your customer roadmap and that means understanding it completely.

How do we expand these intellectual assets within our company? We reward them. We challenge them. Most importantly, we strive daily to consistently acknowledge and partner with them to maximize this hidden potential. Get their feedback—after all, that's why Sherlock Holmes kept Dr. Watson around. It is literally this simple. Just ask your associate if they are working up to their potential. I can attest that anytime I have asked this question, the answer has always surprised me. Go ahead and try it for yourself.

Once you have recognized these crucial achievers, the best way to reward them is with challenges. In fact, history has shown that most people respond positively when given a challenge.

Looking for a Crew

In 1907, Ernest Shackleton was looking for a crew that would sail with him to the South Pole. He put an ad in the *London Times* newspaper that read: "Men wanted for hazardous journey. Low wages. Bitter cold. Long hours of complete darkness. Safe return doubtful. Honor and recognition in the event of success." The next morning 5,000 men lined up outside the London Times building hoping to be one of the crew selected for the trip. The lesson? If a rewarding challenge is given to an employee, and if they visualize their talents meeting this task, you will be witness to a newly energized pulse in your business.

The associates are the first step to partnering within a customer-driven organization. This passionate, motivated staff will deliver better service because you have allowed them to operate on all cylinders. They are problem solvers and add life to your business through creative thinking and an open work environment.

Customers or Partners

Customers today need partners, not puppets. Customer partnerships are a proven strategy for gaining competitive superiority in the marketplace. Not only can you strengthen an existing relationship, customer partnerships have been shown to increase sales, employee productivity, and the bottom-line profitability.

When IKEA was challenged to cut costs from unprofitable products, it determined what its customers truly valued and eliminated elements that didn't matter to them. As a result, they innovated the industry by selling furniture "flat-packed for self-assembly," chopping significant manufacturing, warehousing, and transportation costs.

It is critical when you partner with the customer that you are able to deliver what the customer needs. Ask yourself if there is a better way the organization could be structured or perhaps different ways that operations could be established to deliver the service more efficiently.

I was recently in a line of five people waiting for my local drugstore to open, and there were even more customers waiting in their cars. Three minutes after they were supposed to open, the doors were finally unlocked. This late opening happens frequently at this particular store. I always encourage businesses to open a minimum of ten minutes before their established opening time and close a minimum of ten minutes later than the established closing time if there are still customers in the store. It's a great reminder to bend the rules and let your customers in and not push them out. That is customer partnership, but it takes some staffing commitment and courage to execute.

Major hotels are moving away from the traditional sit-down restaurants and are serving comfort food in upscale fashion. Not long ago, I was meeting a friend at the Hudson Hotel in New York and had a chance to dine at the Hudson Common, which is a "modern-day beer hall and burger joint." They will even send a text when you can pick up your food so you can eat in your room, lounge, or elsewhere. In speaking to one of the managers, he mentioned they partnered with their guests on not only conveniences that would make their experience better, but on the food itself. Don't tell my wife, but that evening I snacked on the white truffle Parmesan popcorn and duck fat fries. The industry standard for restaurant takeout in hotels hovers near 70 percent. The biggest factor that drives sales is convenience and providing a level of food in a manner that is acceptable, easy, and casual. This will be the customer mantra for many years to come.

Don't Tell Them What You're Doing, Tell Them Where You're Going

Why do people get on a train? They get on a train because of three reasons. First, they get on a train because of where it is going. Secondly, they get on a train because of when it is going to arrive. Lastly, they get on a train because they believe, after taking into consideration the cost in terms of time and money, that the cost of the train is worth it. Now just think about if what I said was true. Nobody gets on a train because of where it is. More specifically, nobody gets on a train because of where it is in the station. If you want to have your customers as partners for life or at least a very long time, don't be the train conductor trying to get people to get on a train by saying, "This train is only staying in the station. Come and get on." It won't work. Your customers want to know where your business is going and how it will benefit their lives. They want to go on the ride with you, so take them.

Speaking of rides and partnerships, if you have ever been to Beijing, China, you have probably experienced some of the worst traffic ever. In the spirit of customer partnerships, researchers from Microsoft have been testing a new method for generating faster driving instructions by tapping into the expertise of the local cab drivers and monitoring their GPS trajectories. Current drive time predictions mostly rely on the length of road and posted speed limit. What they learned from the cab drivers in Beijing is they reliably select the fastest path to a destination even if that route might look longer because it takes unexpected side streets. By analyzing GPS data from 33,000 cabs over the course of three months, these researchers were able to determine optimal routes ultimately reducing drive time by 16 percent.

Like any successful relationship, communication is the key driving force behind customer partnering. By fostering this type of environment, you will help ensure that proper expectations are set that will lay the foundation for a long-term relationship. Don't be afraid to ask them how you are doing. This may prevent potential problems from occurring very early in the relationship.

Lastly, gain an understanding why your customers value your services. What do you provide that makes them choose and prefer you over other possible partners? Continue to work on your weaknesses and further develop and focus on your strengths.

Focusing on your strengths directs your talents to what you're good at. Bird hunters know that to kill a lot of birds you do not shoot wildly at a flock in flight. Rather, you aim and shoot one bird, then another, then another—that is, you focus your shooting.

These partnerships are both external and internal. Utilize these same guidelines for your suppliers, vendors, and brokers. It will gain you a competitive advantage.

High jumpers used to always jump facing front, their stomachs traversing the bar. In 1968, Dick Fosbury jumped upside down winning an Olympic gold medal and breaking the high jump record. Now, everyone jumps like that. How can you radicalize your customer partnerships in a world where upside down has become the new right side up?

4

But Don't Always Trust Your Customers to Drive Your Business

"Leaders don't create followers, they create more leaders."

Tom Peters

"Your customer doesn't care how much you know until they know how much you care."

Damon Richards

Across the country, you hear your fair share of talk about what a proponent businesses are of creating customer satisfaction. "We are customer-driven," "We are here to serve your needs," or "We value our customers." Does any of that resemble rhetoric you hear each day or base your service program on? You bet it does. Everybody does it.

It is not that management is unaware of the benefits of a customer-driven business. More accurately, in many instances they do not know how to deliver it. My studies have shown a growing number of organizations are viewing service as a cost rather than an investment. The downside to this is that customers' expectations are on the rise. The distance between the two is wherein lies the problem.

Let me better illustrate this with a story of someone who was watching a crew of 12 park employees get out of their truck. Up and down the parkway they went. Every 20 steps or so six of the employees dug holes and then the other six employees would immediately follow and fill the holes up with dirt again. After about an hour of watching this, the observer could not stand it any longer and he went up to one of the workers and said, "Would you mind telling me what you are doing?" One of them replied, "We're planting trees. The guys with the trees have the day off."

In a customer-driven business, the entire team is working as one unit. They exhibit traits that carry the message from the organization directly to the customers, and they do it consistently. Customer retention is far more advantageous than customer acquisition and this group lives it. Let's examine these characteristics a little closer.

Consistency

Many businesses do things well but seldom do they perform every customer interaction perfectly. This is a challenge for many companies, especially ones that are impacted by numerous transactions within the same experience.

Not long ago, I stayed at a very exquisite hotel overseas. My two days were filled with wonderful customer service, and they made each of my encounters memorable. After checking out and handing the valet my slip to pick up the car, my memorable service ended. They lost the keys. After accusing me of sabotaging their operation, denying they actually ever had the keys, and finally offering to call me a cab to the airport (but not to pay for it mind you), they found the keys a few hours later in the pocket of the valet parker who went home to nap for a few hours. My great service experience was tainted by an unfortunate event—and my last memory of it as well.

Organized Mayhem

It is the trademark of customer-driven organizations. They are energized and inspired to serve the customer. Leadership is fanatic about service and even more so on how it is delivered.

I wish all of you could get a chance to witness what happens when Disney World in Florida closes for the evening.

While you are tucked away resting for the night, an entire army is busy cleaning, painting, landscaping, baking, and countless other chores to make your experience the next day truly a magical one. They are obsessed that no detail is forgotten.

Herb Kelleher, the former CEO of Southwest Airlines, was the poster child for mayhem leadership. He became personally involved in his employees' jobs and even helped the flight attendants serve beverages to customers on the flight. On another occasion when an employee turned down a better paying job offer to stay with Southwest, Herb walked into his office and kissed him. It does not take long for these stories to circulate and build the foundation for which others will follow.

Well Trained

Organizations that are successful at being customer-driven demand training that forms the foundation and soul of the business. All levels receive training, training, and more training. By doing so, they ensure that their customer vision echoes that of all within. In essence, they create the customer-driven behavior they want through this repetitive training.

Customer-Driven without Being Driven Out of Business

The buzz phrase "close to the customer" is the battle cry heard from one coast to the other. In fact, I would be surprised if you have not heard this before at some rally or management address. While it is true that listening to your customers is important, it is even more critical that you look down the road. This is because I have found that customers have little to no vision of your business beyond their current needs.

To further illustrate this point, social psychologist Stanley Milgram conducted an experiment in which he had people stand on the sidewalk and stare up at a window. If one person stood and stared, 40 percent of pedestrians stopped to join in. If two people stared, 60 percent joined, and if five people stared, 90 percent joined—even after the original starer left. It showed you can lead a crowd even when the crowd has no idea that it has a leader, who the leader is, or what the target of the mission was. Call it attraction or cohesion, but customers generally just follow the path of their current needs versus those that lie down the road.

Treating customers as all knowing, all seeing, and all-everything can be a tricky proposition—in fact it can be dangerous. American Airlines learned this when their research indicated that their business traveler wanted more legroom in the coach section of the plane. They ripped out all the seats on their planes, removed a few rows, and reinstalled the seats to give their passengers a few more inches of legroom. American boasted about this new added feature with an advertising campaign and on in-flight messaging. But the new seating plan did not improve sales, and within a few years, they abandoned the program and went back to their previous seating arrangements.

So you ask, what happened? Well, American learned that while extending the legroom was a nice feature for their business customers, it added little to nothing to their customers' overall satisfaction. Rather, passengers were more concerned about pricing (which went up when they took those seats out) and scheduling. The lesson—find out what truly matters to your customers and react accordingly.

A few months ago, I was asked to observe a business that had brought in three top customers to gain a better understanding of what they felt the future direction of the company should be. After listening to their comments over the period of two days, I came to the conclusion they had no idea what they wanted. Yes, they were able to provide useful feedback, but most were minor irrational improvements that would not propel the business forward past the customers' daily concerns.

A short time later, we addressed the general managers within this business and posed the same questions. Ironically, what I saw was a consistent message that provided solutions to their current needs and strategies to provide long-term vitality. As a result, they combined the useful short-term feedback of the customers with the future vision of the general managers to create a customer-driven environment that would survive for years to come.

One of my favorite quotes of all time came from Henry Ford. He was spot-on when he said, "If I had asked people what they wanted, they would have said faster horses." Another one I enjoy comes from Malcolm Gladwell who said, "When you ask people what coffee they prefer, they say a 'dark, rich hearty roast,' when you see what they actually drink, it's a milky weak coffee." It serves as an example that people can explain only what they think they want. They can share their rational desires without ever realizing that when it comes time to make a choice, they may choose very differently. Asking consumers their opinions can be problematic as they make choices outside of their conscious awareness in favor of familiar items.

Hidden Dangers in Giving Customers What They Want

Customers are not technology wizards, futurists, or even visionaries of your business. For example, if you asked farmers in the 1800s what they wanted, they would have said, "A horse that is twice as strong and eats half as much." Most likely they wouldn't have replied, "How about making me a tractor?" Customers can offer excellent feedback for improving existing products and services, but can perform miserably when solicited for ideas that depart from the norm.

Scientist and philosopher Arthur Schopenhauer said it best, "The task is not so much to see what no one yet has seen, but to think what nobody yet has thought about that which everybody sees." When Coca-Cola's research indicated that people preferred the taste of Pepsi, they rushed out a new product very quickly. New Coke failed for multiple reasons, but mainly because researchers were answering questions in controlled labs using their conscious minds. This drove misleading results and the ultimate failure of New Coke. The best way to research customers' selection will always be in their natural environment—whether that's your store, business, or where they purchase the product.

In many instances, customers do not know they need a new product or service until they see it. A great example of this would be 3M, who is the innovator of such successes as Scotchgard and Post-its. They often research chemical compounds with no specific customer needs in mind.

Businesses must be careful not to be so focused on today's customers that they forget about tomorrow's customers. IBM learned this the hard way. In 1960–1970, they owned a 70 percent market share in mainframes. You may recall their motto, "IBM means service." They were so concerned about taking care of their top customers that they maintained a fleet of Learjets to fly technical personnel to the major customers. Unfortunately, while they took care of their top customers, IBM was not looking at their customer needs in the future and missed the move to microcomputers.

Finding the Balance

Today, it is critical to find the balance between being technology driven versus customer-service driven. If you are entirely technology driven, you stand the chance of promoting products that customers may not be interested in. If you are customer-service driven, you may be so close to your existing customers that you may be passed by your competition, who is looking ahead.

Like Butch Cassidy in that famous movie, businesses must continually ask, "Who are these people and why are they after us?" What could we have done to avoid these problems? But that misses the point. The customers are not concerned about your economic or technological challenges or balances. Remember, customers have the final say on what they want, but not where you should go. Determine what your company stands for and be the best at it. Just as Jaguar doesn't build inexpensive compacts, Frito-Lay doesn't make cereal, and Burger King doesn't serve tacos, the same logic applies to your business as you stay incredibly focused on your customer.

5

Death by 1,000 Paper Cuts

"I don't have pet peeves like some people. I have whole kennels of irritation."

Whoopi Goldberg

"We see our customers as invited guests to a party, and we are the hosts. It's our job every day to make every important aspect of the customer experience a little bit better."

Jeff Bezos

Mel Brooks has always been known for his unusual sense of humor and ability to make us see a little part of ourselves in his films. I cannot help but think of a scene in his film *Blazing*

Saddles where a new sheriff is appointed in a small town in the late 1800s. It's a town of narrow-minded bigots who are opposed to anything out of the ordinary. The new sheriff is black and none of the townspeople want to accept him, so they decide to kill him. As all the townsmen simultaneously pull out their guns to kill the newcomer, the sheriff pulls out his own gun, puts it to his head and says, "Come any closer and the sheriff's dead!" The townsmen slowly back away, afraid the sheriff might kill the sheriff. It makes no sense, but the sheriff managed to outsmart the townspeople.

How does this humorous example parallel our own actions when it comes to understanding customer irritants? Many times, despite good intentions, our own tactics often backfire on us. While we think we are being wise by generating an extra penny or two from our customers, we often distance ourselves further from them. Organizations that lack a commonsense approach are prone to being the biggest violators.

When McDonald's was tinkering with a new way to improve service at its location in Chicago's Midway Airport, it adopted a new point of sale system that put LARGE order numbers on every receipt. This allowed customers to step away from the counter and return when their numbers were called. A win-win as the customers could wait peacefully and confidently well away from the chaos of the busy counter and McDonald's could generate more business with the freed-up space. When testing this in their innovation center, staff even hauled in their own luggage to simulate the airport experience.

Make it Easy

So what does "make it easy" mean for your frontline associates? In most instances, they would tell you making it easy for the customer would be where they'd start. And that starts with removing obstacles. Forget all the bells and whistles and just solve your customer's problems.

Customer service is not only what you do for your customers, it is also what you don't do. It is about removing barriers and obstacles that detract from a customer's experience. In most cases, these irritants are easily correctable and relatively inexpensive to eliminate.

In Boston, I stayed at a nice downtown hotel but arrived very late in the evening. After getting settled in my room, I called down for a wake-up call (I know, I'm the only one that still does that) and immediately got the hotel's voice mail system. "Thanks for calling the 'name withheld.' To ensure each guest's call is handled appropriately, please listen to the following options. To book a meeting room for ten or more guest rooms, please dial 1. For guest room reservations, please dial 2. If you signed an event contract and need to speak to your event specialist, please dial 3. For information about a corporate rate, please dial 4. For a guest service representative, please dial 0 or stay on the line."

Now, when do you think the last time was that a leader at that hotel listened to their in-room guest voicemail? If I am calling from a room, I do not need the first 4 prompts.

In addition, if I hit 0 to start the call, why have me listen to all those prompts to only have to push 0 again at the end?

Killing Me Softly—The True Cost of Irritants

In my lifetime, I have flown in excess of a million miles and have stayed in more than 500 domestic and foreign hotels/resorts. One common irritant that disturbs me is the added charge for Wi-Fi that many of these properties bill their guests. It is amazing that you can pay $275 for a room and still be expensed for utilizing the available Wi-Fi service.

You're probably saying, "Brian, they make substantial revenue from these charges." I accept that, but wouldn't it make more sense for them to tack an extra dollar or two onto the room rate and eliminate the surcharge? Think of the goodwill that would create. As I write this some 30,000 feet in the air, the passenger next to me just related that she stayed in a mid-priced hotel chain the previous evening, which had eliminated this charge. Who knows, maybe they are waking up and smelling the coffee.

Speaking of coffee, I was in the Atlanta airport and wanted a small coffee but requested a large cup so as not to spill on my laptop. The young cashier behind the counter stated that she would have to charge me for a large. I told her nicely that I didn't want a large coffee but requested a large cup to prevent an accident. Her reply was "Maybe it would be better for you to buy a small coffee and I will only fill that halfway up." Although this appeared upsetting at the time, I certainly do not hold this associate at fault. Obviously, somebody on the management team had directed her to charge by the cup, not by the coffee. This may make perfect sense to this business, but it irritated and lost this customer (me) who now goes 50 feet farther down the concourse to get my small coffee served in a large cup.

One of the biggest irritants I personally experience and am asked about is long checkout lines. Staffing is tight especially in light of challenging sales. However, the front-end should be the last place you will want to pull back on payroll. According to a report by PricewaterhouseCoopers (PwC), 28 percent of consumers make purchases based on convenience. The report goes on to say that in terms of convenience, fast lines matter even more than location and self-checkouts. In fact, fast checkouts account for 30 percent of memorable great experiences. Armed with this information, that getting in and out quickly is a key priority for their customers, retailers must ensure that customers have short wait times.

A different take on short wait times was a challenge the Houston airport faced a few years ago. Passengers were lodging significant quantities of complaints about the long wait time at baggage claim. So the executives increased the number of baggage handlers working and wait times were reduced slightly, but the complaints continued to pour in.

Confused, the airport executives took a more careful, on-site analysis and found that it took passengers a minute to walk from their arrival gates to baggage claim and seven more minutes to get their bags. Almost 88 percent of their time, in other words, was spent standing around waiting for their bags.

So the airport took a new approach: rather than reducing wait times, they moved the arrival gates away from the main terminal and routed bags to the farthest carousel. Passengers now had to walk six times longer to get their bags. Complaints dropped to almost zero.

It's the same logic on why you find mirrors next to elevators today. The idea was actually born during the post-World War II boom, when high-rises popped up at an alarming rate and led to complaints about elevator delays. Similar to the Houston airport example, the mirrors gave people something to occupy their time, whether that was looking at their outfit or checking out others. As a result, the wait felt shorter and their complaints diminished. Both offered clever ways to reduce irritants.

Retailers should be extremely concerned when they create these self-inflicted irritations among customers. Strategies need to be developed for eliminating irritants. What is the best way to discover if irritants are prevalent in your business? Easy. Be a customer.

Walk your sales floor. Look at your signs that are posted. Call your Web site or .com line. Ask questions of your department heads and cashiers. When you put on the glasses of a customer instead of a manager or associate, you may be surprised at what you see. I hope it is a pleasant surprise, but if not, at a minimum you have recognized a potential irritant and can now take the necessary steps to correct it.

Royal Caribbean got criticized via social feedback and guest satisfaction surveys that their guests often struggled to find a crew member when they needed basic assistance. So now, they augment their crew with interactive kiosks on every deck of their new ships. These kiosks answer two of the most often asked questions they get from their guests. "What activities are happening now?" and "How the heck do I get back to my room?"

Not very long ago, I purchased a laptop for my son from a local electronics store. Within a short period of time, it was not working properly and since it was still under warranty, I called the service center. The first three hours I was unable to get a person due to a busy signal. When I finally did get through, it was answered by an annoying recording that repeated each minute by telling me how valuable I was and how it would be answered in the order it was received. This message played 24 times before a customer-service person picked up.

After taking my information, she told me the earliest she could send out a technician to the house would be seventeen days later. I reminded the customer-service rep what it stated on the back of my receipt.

> *Should a product covered by the manufacturer's in-home service warranty fail, we will dispatch a service technician to promptly and properly repair defective products to the manufacturer's specifications at no charge.*

She replied to me, "Seventeen days falls within the window of prompt." Not done, she finished that with "Do you want me to send the technician or don't you?"

Needless to say, I had the CEO of this company on the telephone with me the following day. With him on the telephone along with me, I attempted to conference in the service center and guess what? You got it. The line was busy. When we finally did get through, he kept quiet as the customer-service representative teed off on me. Two days later, a new laptop was delivered to my house.

This CEO had absolutely no idea how irritated his customers were by the systems in place at this organization. Only after he experienced it as "a customer," did he begin to see just how broken it really was. One more thing, this chain went out of business shortly after that experience.

RFID Can Help

Many businesses are starting to use RFID to improve and simplify the experience by eliminating irritants that customers had identified. If you're not familiar with RFID, it's a type of wireless technology that lets you identify objects that have been fitted with special RF identification tags. While cost continues to play a role in the adoption of RFID, its benefits are felt by consumers on a daily basis. Here are some examples of the beneficial use of RFID tags:

- **Libraries**: *when books are fitted with RFID tags, piles or rows of books on a shelf can be* *quickly scanned without having to move or rearrange them.*

- **Passports:** *becoming more common and allows faster entry into a country.*

- **Smart Fitting Rooms:** *several retailers started outfitting dressing rooms with interactive, RFID-powered kiosks. By scanning dressing room items, shoppers can access product data, find similar alternatives, and provide feedback. On my last trip to London, I was afforded the opportunity to utilize the "Magic Mirror" at Burberry, where RFID technology let me see a 360-degree view of the jacket I was trying on. Why go to all this fuss? How about the fact that 67 percent of customers who try on items buy them. That's why stores have begun to make changing rooms more attractive and exciting to customers. The dressing room is where emotion happens with a product. A display can make a customer fall in love with an item, but when they can try it on in a beautifully furnished, bright and clean fitting room, then, more importantly, they fall in love with the item—on themselves instead of the mannequin. Sorry about the rant, but what an amazing sales opportunity this little area can be.*

- **Animal identification**: *RFID ear tags used for cattle or to register and find a lost dog.*

- **Toll Roads**: *The sensors allow very fast identification and exchange of other information.*

- **Amusement Parks**: *Disney integrated RFID technology into their tickets. The credit-card style tickets eliminate the need for scanning and swiping in ride lines, reducing wait times, and lowering staffing costs. Additionally, the RFID-enabled tickets provide park operators a rich source of information for tracking the movement of thrill-seekers throughout the grounds.*

- **Sports**: *Sick of losing golf balls like I am? Ready to swing away and not worry about trying to see your ball that went into the woods? A number of specialized sporting good providers have introduced RFID golf balls.*

- **Car Rental**: *Not long ago, I had an early morning flight where the rental car company was not staffed. No problem! Since this was Avis and the car was RFID equipped, I was able to park in any open spot and go.*

- *Medical Applications: For example, providing patients with a wristband that contains the patient's identity and information relating to the patient's medical condition. Hospital applications include tracking and recording of drugs and samples. A startup called First Hand Hygiene is looking to make its RFID-enabled mark by addressing the simple but serious problem of getting health-care workers to wash their hands. The technology is elegantly simple: Workers wear a wristband and RFID readers are positioned by the faucets. It's reliable, unobtrusive, and less expensive than paying a squad of moms to follow nurses and doctors around! Now that's eliminating an irritant.*

Eliminate Internal Irritants

My wife is a registered nurse. One of the prevalent concerns she hears from executives to nurses are irritants that develop when staffing problems occur.

A William M. Mercer survey of Human Resource executives in 185 health-care organizations nationwide found that increase in market demand and workload (not pay) were the top two reasons for registered nurse turnover. Now armed with that information, health-care executives should be looking at eliminating RN irritants, such as improper alignment between clinical and operational procedures, poor training, improper skill mix, and too many patients.

With RN turnover extremely costly, it is in management's best interest to work with them to remove internal irritants and improve these strained relationships. Hendrie Weisinger, the author of *Anger at Work: Learning the Art of Anger Management on the Job,* reports that most working people experience some level of annoyance at least ten times a day. If an organization can eliminate at least 50 percent of these, just think how much happier the associates and your customers will be as a result of it.

There is an old Chinese adage that goes something like this. "A man must sit in a chair with his mouth open a long time before a roast duck will fly in." If you want roast duck, i.e., if you want to eliminate irritants both for your customers and employees, you must go hunting for it yourself.

6

Listen Up and You Shall Grow

"Look out for the fellow who lets you do all the talking."

Kin Hubbard

"Traditional corporations, particularly large-scale service and manufacturing businesses are organized for efficiency. Or consistency. But not joy. If you fear special requests, if you staff with cogs, if you have to put it all in a manual, then the chances of amazing someone are really quite low."

Seth Godin

1. Write down any 3-digit number. (The number cannot mirror itself, e.g., don't use 323, 565, etc.)

2. *Reverse the number you just wrote down, then subtract the lower/smaller number from the higher/larger number. [If the subtraction yielded a 2-digit number (99), add a zero in front of it (099).]*

3. *Now, reverse the result and add it to the preceding answer/result. I will share the answer to the above problem at the end of the chapter, and you'll understand why I included this little exercise in the book.*

Does anyone seem to listen anymore? It's no wonder they don't as we are bombarded with voices urging us to buy, vote, go here, and spend there. From our homes to our workplaces, we are surrounded by people who have something to say. In our society, listening is an undervalued activity and therefore goes almost basically unrecognized. Listening does not make any noise and appears to be intangible. Talk is heard.

So, why aren't we good listeners? First, listening is mistakenly equated with hearing and since most of us can hear, little value is placed on it. In fact, time experts have shown we spend 9 percent of our day typing/writing, 16 percent reading, 30 percent speaking, and 45 percent listening. Just the opposite of our academic system.

Secondly, many perceive power in talking. Those who have the ability of good speech are often perceived as more valuable.

When you compare speech to listening in the eyes of your customers, they would rather be heard than spoken to. Listening is not just with your ears alone, but also with your eyes, posture, facial expression, and overall general demeanor. Businesses must recognize that listening is not passive, but rather an active mode of communication.

Michael P. Nichols, author of *The Lost Art of Listening*, says, "Few motives in human experience are as powerful as the yearning to be understood. Being listened to means that we are taken seriously, that our ideas and feelings are known, and, ultimately, that what we have to say matters."

All too often, the talking is coming from the CEO and other upper executive personnel. Improving the customer-service program is as easy as listening to both customers and associates. West Point teacher and legendary World War I General "Black Jack" Pershing stated that the first rule of leadership is "Listening to the privates." Top management stands a far greater chance of connecting with the customers by listening to their needs. My wife is a retired Captain in the United States Navy. She had an amazing relationship with her hospital corpsmen, partially because she always afforded them respect, but more importantly, because she was an amazing listener when that skill was needed.

Listening Can Do More Good Than We Realize

An Alaskan once told a friend he did not believe in God. When asked why, he launched into a story about being lost in the wilderness.

"I was in total despair. I prayed to God to rescue me."

"Well, you're here," said the friend. "Doesn't that prove that God exists?"

"Are you kidding?" said the Alaskan. "Some Eskimo came along and showed me the way out."

By human nature, people do not listen to what is said, but rather what they want to hear. Poor listening skills while interacting with a customer can lead to frustration. To avoid this, the associate must be careful not to fill in the gray areas themselves by assuming they knew what the customer meant. If there is still confusion after the exchange, then you are not finished and need to get further clarification from the customer.

An old adage says good salespeople are "blessed with the gift of gab." Unfortunately, customers prefer talking to listening. As a result, sales are lost and relationships are wounded. Focus on listening and understanding. Do not attempt to sell. If you listen, understand, and answer your customers' questions, they will sell themselves on your products and services.

Toss the Ball Back

I am a long-time, die-hard, extremely frustrated Chicago Cubs fan. One of the traditions at the friendly confines known as Wrigley Field is for the fans to toss the ball back onto the field after the opponent hits a home run. Let's look at how we can apply good listening skills to this example.

Envision a conversation with a customer as a game of catch. Every time you are talking, you have the ball. While you are holding the ball, you are unable to acquire information or better understand the customer because you are talking. The longer you have the ball, the less the customer is heard.

We want to throw the ball back to our customers as soon as possible. To accomplish that, you may have to ask them a question. When your customer holds the ball, they are relaying information and important feedback that can be beneficial.

There is a joke about a famous psychiatrist who is approached at a cocktail party by a solicitous guest. "My dear doctor, how can you stand to listen to people's problems all day long? It must be dreadfully depressing." Somewhat taken aback by the man's provocative question, but determined not to be easily annoyed, the psychiatrist quips, "Listen? Who listens?"

In a survey by the Coleman Consulting Group involving 22,000 shift workers in various American industries, 70 percent revealed that there is little communication with plant and company management; 59 percent said they believe their company really doesn't care about them. In other words, nobody is listening.

Listening to Your Customers Is Better Than Trying to Educate Them

Your customers don't work for you. They already have full-time jobs, families, and commitments. Don't assume that if your customers simply had more knowledge about your business their behavior would change. Knowledge doesn't always guarantee behavior change. For behavior to change, your customer has to understand what's in it for them in a very simple and straightforward fashion.

Changing customer behavior isn't about educating them, it's about the experiences you offer that they see as making their life easier, better, and more efficient, to name a few. The iPhone comes without a user manual, and it might be the most complicated device the public has ever used.

Customers are like the duck that wanted grapes. If you haven't heard that story, a duck waddles into a convenience store, hops on the counter, and says to the guy there, "Got any grapes?" The guy says, "I'm sorry. We don't have any grapes." The duck nods, hops off the counter and waddles out. The next day, the duck comes back in, hops on the counter and asks, "Got any grapes?" The guy sighs and says, "Let me explain. This is a convenience store. We don't carry any produce. So no, I don't have any grapes." Again, the duck nods, hops off the counter and waddles out. Back he comes the next day, hops onto the counter and asks, "Got any grapes?" Now the guy is exasperated. "Listen, I explained to you that this store doesn't carry grapes. And if you ask me one more time I'll nail those stupid feet of yours to the counter." The duck nods, hops down, and waddles out. The next day, the duck waddles in again, hops on the counter, and asks, "Got any nails?" The guy behind the counter takes a deep breath and says, "You would really need to find a hardware store for that. No, I don't have any nails." The duck nods and says, "Good. Got any grapes?"

That duck was not going to be educated about convenience stores and your customer is not going to be educated on the inner workings and challenges of your business. That is the equivalent of trying to educate your customers on the different channels they can engage you on. Don't bother, as customers don't see channels, they see experiences. The guy in the convenience store was never going to get rid of the persistent duck by educating it. His effort would have been better spent trying to figure out why the darned thing wanted grapes in the first place.

Broken Windows Theory

The theory goes something like this: higher crime rates occur in cities when broken windows are left unrepaired because people conclude no one cares enough to fix them. This can parallel a retailer that does not put enough care into ensuring their bathrooms are properly cleaned for associates let alone customers. Or poor staffing analytics that leave fitting rooms disorganized or not recovered during peak business and the evening associate is charged with the monumental task to get it all put away. Associates will help you understand these pain points if you simply ask.

Organizations must engage with their associates. Think of "engage" in the mechanical sense, the way gears work on a car. When you push in the clutch and engage the gear, the car begins to move. When you engage in a conversation, you don't just talk you listen.

At the beginning of the chapter, I asked you to follow a set of instructions. If you followed them correctly, you will have the answer 1089 no matter what three-digit number you started with. Listening is very much like that. It doesn't matter very much how or where you start. It's where you want to go that is important. As a reductionist, my best secret for being a good listener is simply to close my mouth—and listen.

Age of the Consumer—Buzz Phrase for the 21st Century

"In just two days, tomorrow will be yesterday."

> *Anonymous*

"Make the customer the hero of your story."

> *Ann Handley*

A man lived through the terrible Johnstown flood and spent the rest of his life talking about his experience. He became so eloquent that he turned professional and toured the country lecturing before huge crowds. Eventually, he died and went to heaven. He had no sooner gotten settled in when he began to pester St. Peter about giving one of his lectures.

After a few days passed, St. Peter said to him, "It's all set. We have reserved an auditorium for you that will seat 10,000, and I expect every seat to be taken. But there is one thing you must know before you give your speech on the flood. One person who will be in attendance will be a man named Noah."

That story should give you a good idea of what it is like to speak to experts. In your case, these experts are your customers. Generation after generation that knows what it is to be a customer. Most are knowledgeable with regards to products and services. Those who reign successful in the 21st century will understand this and utilize their customers like never before. Let's delve into this a little deeper.

"The Deer Now Have All the Guns"

Consumers have quickly become better at harnessing technology and using it to their advantage and currently outpace retailers who are still trying to react to it. Today, instead of being "hunted," consumers have become the "hunters." They have the "guns" via their mobile devices that can check prices, shop web sites, and control their shopping experience. They expect to be able to interact within the retail environment with their mobile device. In many instances, your associates have less information than their customers. So while the game continues to evolve, the challenge for retailers and businesses is to figure out how to best serve their customers across all channels.

Today's customers are unlike any the retail industry has ever seen. They have in their hands more information and more capabilities than we could have ever imagined. While the customer has always been the center of the universe, they are now transforming the landscape and changing the rules. In spite of this or rather as a result of it, retailers are now provided an incredible opportunity to get more engaged with their customers via this technology. Just as you can't clean a house while you're not in it, it's equally important that you ensure your associates have as much information or at least the tools to secure the information needed to satisfy the customer.

The age of the consumer can be seen in significant shifts that have taken place in recent years. They have completely altered how we get from a to b, how we buy, and even where we sleep. Just think, Uber, the worlds largest taxi company owns no vehicles. Facebook, the world's most popular media owner, creates no content. Alibaba, the most valuable retailer, has no inventory. As of today, Airbnb is the world's largest accommodation provider yet owns no real estate.

Currently, there is a massive untapped resource available in our customer base. Businesses should harness this potential and find ways to continually involve their customers in every facet of their business plan. It is quite simple, actually.

If your customers represent nothing more than dollars to you, their only existence to your business is price. However, if you can channel their passion and give them more reasons than price alone to do business with you, then you begin to foster a relationship that has vitality as it moves forward.

Empowerment of consumers is important to the life of a business because it contributes to the formation of lasting relationships. Think of these relationships as a marriage. How healthy would it be if only one spouse brought context and love to the marriage? Relationships, like a good marriage, involve mutual exchanges of thoughts and ideas. Your customers are no different.

At St. Joseph's University in Philadelphia, I had the opportunity to participate in an exercise where store directors from a retail food corporation were given copies of their top 100 shoppers by name and the amount of dollars spent weekly. Each store director was asked to evaluate the list to determine how many of their top 10 customers they recognized. It was interesting to watch as the unofficial total was only about 5 percent of the top ten customers were known by the store directors. That means of the 1,500 or so "best customers," only 75 were known to these store directors.

After this exercise, the store directors were asked to go back to their stores, contact their customers, and thank them for their business. Many invited these customers to introduce themselves the next time they were shopping and rewarded them with a cake, gift certificates, or other tokens of appreciation. Several store directors commented that they recognized the top customers once they met them but never knew their name or guessed how much they spent in their stores.

Armed with this information, they have now fostered a relationship with their top 10 shoppers. Now these customers know they are recognized and now offer important input that is valued to the management team.

Think about the lifetime value of these customers. They might not make the biggest purchases, but they're the ones that come back again and again. Contrast this to a traditional sales approach that can be likened to pouring customers into a bucket with a hole in the bottom—the weaker your levels of customer retention the larger the hole.

My direction to them was don't stop there. Contact the next ten and the next ten and the next . . .

Now, more than ever, the concept of customer empowerment is changing. Customers today are branded with products and services that are identical or differentiated very little from business to business. The customer of tomorrow will represent the company. The products and services will reflect the company and enhance the personal relationship they enjoy with their customers. If you cannot personalize this relationship, it will be useless. "Dear Customer" is the kiss of death. Everything you communicate to your customer should explain how the product or service will improve his or her life, not what the features are.

As a result, the big winner in the 21st century is the customer. Organizations that cater to their customers with individualized/personalized service will be the victors.

Without this personalized service, there is no loyalty, thus no reasons for the customers to come back. However, heed my warning. Empowered customers will also be demanding customers. Shoppers have a myriad of choices and will exploit your weaknesses much more than a customer where no relationship exists. Fostering customer relationships helps promote loyalty.

Procter & Gamble discovered how rewarding these customer relationships could be when it introduced Physique, a new line of hair-care products. They utilized research that examined both demographic and psychological trends. It brilliantly identified the "chatters" or consumers that are effective at influencing others about hot new products. Samples were sent directly to these consumers and a web site that encouraged visitors to tell a friend was also aimed at this group. The results? The marketing program generated in excess of 1 million referrals to the Physique web site in just a few months. Although unheard of at the time, less than 15 percent of Physique's marketing dollars went to television advertising. Physique is not sold anymore, but this strategy remains the hallmark beginning of social marketing.

Procter & Gamble has evolved and no longer relies solely on internal research and development to generate new product ideas. They tap into their customers who identify needs for a new product. Their researchers then take that idea and prepare a technology brief that is released to a network of technology entrepreneurs. This customer-centric thinking has produced the Swiffer, Crest SpinBrush, and Olay Regenerist.

This is a trend that will persevere. The Internet and electronic commerce will continue to reduce the costs of marketing and doing business on the international level. That means even small and medium-size businesses can now compete with large organizations. Technology will continue to shrink markets down to the size of the individual customer. That is why customer empowerment will be the factor driving customer-driven businesses.

Expectations Drive Everything

Customer expectations aren't right or wrong, good or bad, in or out, or high or low. They just are. Service and satisfaction are in the eye of the beholder and the beholder sets expectations. However, some businesses have no idea what the customers expect. How can you meet and/or exceed their expectations if you don't even know what their expectations are?

In an Egg and Bacon Breakfast, What's the Difference between the Chicken and the Pig?

Having had the opportunity to speak with domestic and international businesses, I have witnessed increased success in those that placed an emphasis on customer empowerment delivering on expectations. Retaining high-value customers while delivering more service to existing customers can be a powerful weapon in your arsenal. But that means you must be all-in on this approach—no room to dance and jive and sometimes play in that space. You need to be staunch, dedicated, and devoted to building and maintaining those customer relationships. The results will amaze you. If you ever need a reminder, just remember the answer to the riddle: The Chicken is involved, but the Pig is committed!

8

Never Put Your Team in a Square Boat

"In a time of drastic change, the learners will inherit the future. Those who have finished learning find themselves equipped to live in a world that no longer exists."
Eric Hoffer

"The person who is not hungry says the coconut has a hard shell."
African Proverb

A premier sculling coach took his team to a race. After practicing for weeks and preparing intensely, they lost. Following the race, they returned home and the coach decided they needed their morale lifted, so he threw a party and gave them the next two days off. At the next race, they lost again.

These losses mounted over the next several weeks until the coach became so frustrated he decided he had lost his touch and contemplated retirement. In a desperate last-ditch move, he had the boat removed from the water so he could examine it. Once removed, the problem became quite evident. The hull had been poorly constructed and was producing a strong drag on its forward movement. More specifically, the team was trying to win in a square boat.

The same principle applies to developing customer-service teams. Managers and supervisors, like the coach, sometimes forget their role includes examining the boat. In other words, recognize that it is certainly easier to blame associates' work and low morale than it is to explore the real reasons for their failure. No matter how talented a team is, without the proper design, they are operating at a disadvantage.

Enthusiasm Is Not Enough

The knight was returning to the castle after a long hard day. His face was bruised and badly swollen. His armor was dented. The plume on his helmet was broken and his steed was limping. He was a sad sight.

The lord of the castle came running out and asked, "What hath befallen you, Sir Timothy?"

"Oh Sire," he said, "I have been laboring all day in your service, bloodying and pillaging your enemies to the West."

"You've been doing WHAT?" asked the lord.

Thinking the man must be a little deaf, Timothy repeated what he had said but much louder.

"But I haven't any enemies to the West," was the reply.

"Oh!" said Timothy, followed by, "Well, I think you do now."

There is a moral to this little story and that is enthusiasm is not enough. Associates need a sense of direction. They want to understand the end-to-end process and this will position them to better deliver on your goals. Failure is usually not caused by lack of enthusiasm, but enthusiasm by itself is not near enough. If you hired correctly, associates' level of enthusiasm can be infectious, and it can motivate teams to do great things. However, without a clear plan, all of the motivation can end up being channeled in the wrong way. As the Chinese general Sun Tzu said, "He will win whose army is animated by the same spirit through all ranks." Alignment does not mean issuing precise instructions but rather ensuring that everyone in the organization understands the needs of the business and works to deliver on those goals. Remember, if the coach did nothing to rebuild the hull, then he is still left with a square boat. Recognizing a faulty design in your customer-service team is just the first step. The real challenge is your willingness to do something about it. That may include securing capital to arm them with the latest technology. Or possibly ridding the business of old and outdated operating policies. A new app by Openbay Connect is going after the outdated business practice of waiting until your check engine light goes on or a mechanical breakdown occurs before getting your car fixed. Their service aims to tell drivers about breakdowns before they happen and automatically get bids on the repairs from local service shops. The free app reads alerts from the onboard computers and the driver doesn't have to lift a finger. It even provides the driver with a diagnosis, guaranteed price, service time, and ratings on the repair shops.

Finding New Ways to Help Fans

Football fans from all over the tri-state area love to sit in the stands at Lincoln Financial Field and watch their Philadelphia Eagles football team. When I lived in Philadelphia, this experience was part of my every other Sunday routine. The Director of Event Operations at the time was Leonard Bonacci, whose job was to ensure the fan experience was an excellent one as tickets are by no means cheap. If there is one thing to know about the Philadelphia Eagles fans, they are passionate about their team and I am being kind. You may recall this is the group that booed and pelted Santa Claus at halftime.

Part of Leonard's role was to quickly resolve disagreements such as a fan using profanity, blocking another persons view, or countless other annoyances. With some 70,000 fans attending a game and over 1.5 million square feet of football stadium to watch over, the job became too big for Leonard and his relatively small team.

He realized that he could serve the fans better if he empowered them to assist. So he enabled spectators to use text messaging to alert his team about disturbances in the crowd. The tickets and seat signs directed fans to text-message a 5-digit code to get help. This program proved to be so successful that every National Football League stadium now utilizes it. In fact, you would be hard-pressed to attend any major sporting event and not see this new approach. Leonard applied existing technology in an unheard of and creative way to solve a customer problem.

Choosing the Right Team

In my school days, it was relatively easy picking the right team. All you had to do was look at them. The big husky guys were always the first to get picked for the tackle football games while the less athletic ones were sent to the other team. Unfortunately, surrounding yourself with a winning service team these days takes careful planning and becomes a little more complicated than picking those grammar school superstars.

When I assemble a customer-service team, I look for five traits that will give me a competitive advantage. Let's examine these.

There Is No 'I' in Team

We already talked about the whole team being stronger than the sum of its parts. This was never illustrated better than it was in the movie classic, *It's a Wonderful Life*, starring Jimmy Stewart. It is shown every holiday season. In it, our hero is so desperate over losses at the bank, he runs and resolves to take his own life. An angel appears and reveals what the future of his town will be if no local lender exists. The well-being of the community hangs on the frail thread of this man and his willingness to hold together the community lending institution. Our hero chooses life and returns home to find that the entire town has contributed small amounts of cash to bridge the deficit. No single one of them could have saved the bank, but together, the town saved itself.

When assembling a team, it is just that—a team and not an individual with a supporting cast. It is important that the talent and resources of various individuals are utilized to their greatest potential for the benefit of your customers.

One-Stop Shopping

Flattening the organization will result in fewer layers for the team thus reducing time and energy associated with approvals and bureaucracy. That means the team needs to be multifunctional and skilled in all areas of the decision-making process.

Hire, train, and reward associates that demonstrate the ability to function across different areas. Like a football game, the fewer handoffs, the less of a chance there is to fumble the ball.

Motivated Team Members

Let's face it. These days, businesses are trying to deliver increased service levels while reducing costs at the same time. As a result, a different and unique type of team member is required. An associate who thrives on challenges such as solving problems or taking on new skills will be in high demand. The traditional employee who requires consistent direction and is unable to make decisions will be left behind.

Motivation is key to helping support your high performance team members. The fun and positive environment you surround your people in is crucial in strengthening morale and the team itself. Don't ever minimize the importance of associates who deliver a friendly experience. "Nice makes more money," according to psychologist Daniel Goleman, whose research indicates that business revenues increase 1 percent for every 2 percent increase in "service climate," the phrase for how friendly and helpful a company's employees act.

Don't Hire Yourself

Sometimes, when we look to summon a team together, we are prone to having that team resemble ourselves. That may not always be what's best as that person who is unlike ourselves may be better suited for the team than we are. Different personalities, talents, and views all contribute to the uniqueness of the team. I have witnessed on numerous occasions customer-service teams that on paper looked odd but worked together like a well-tuned piano.

Problem-Solving Skills

This skill is critical because what is the point of voicing a concern to a business if they are not prepared to help solve the problem? That means your team will really need to have a strong understanding of your product and service to be able to address the concern more quickly. This is where that listening skill that was addressed in the prior chapter really comes into play.

When 1 + 1 + 1 Does Not Equal 3

Best-in-class companies learn how to deliver great experiences by optimizing their associates and the experience they deliver throughout the customer journey and not just at individual touchpoints. Individual touchpoints may yield good results but the overall experience may not add up.

For example, when we were considering switching from one Internet provider to another, that journey spanned about 30 days, involved more than six phone calls and ultimately a visit to our home by the technician. At each of those touchpoints, I would describe the experience as pretty good. The service providers on the phone were polite and were able to either answer my question or transfer me to someone that could. The technician that came to my home was very knowledgeable, respectful, and showed up on time. However, as I looked at the total experience, I was much less satisfied. Why did I have to make six phone calls? Several of those calls during the process were attempts to clarify additional product information. Couldn't that have been handled on their web site or in the promotional materials? Most of the individual interactions I would have rated between a 7 and 10, but when I look back at the experience as a whole, I would rate it as a 4 out of 10. Although most of these service encounters were very positive, the underlying problems could have been avoided and the ultimate journey in this process could have been much better.

When you think about your customer experience, don't limit yourself to just the touchpoints. This narrow focus will never allow you to see the customer journey through their eyes. In this multichannel, multi-device, multi-touchpoint world we operate in, this focus makes delivering on the customer journey difficult. No doubt about it. But if you can engage with your customers at every level within their journey—staying close by getting out into the stores, listening to phone calls in the call center, and reviewing social media posts—then you will stand a much greater chance of witnessing the end-to-end experience. Remember, not all customers take the same journey, so no single solution will be the answer. Don't miss the customer journey by only focusing on the individual experiences. Great customer service is a story, not just a long road of touchpoints.

9

Let's Get Engaged!

"To win in the marketplace you must first win in the workplace."
> Doug Conant

"The key is to set realistic customer expectations, and then not to just meet them, but to exceed them—preferably in unexpected and helpful ways."
> Richard Branson

The shopping experience today can be one of self-checkouts and store visits where we rarely encounter a member of the team. When we participate in a loyalty program, we are not met with smiles, but with coupons or a card. Americans hold more than 3.3 billion loyalty program memberships according to the 2015 Colloquy Loyalty Census or roughly 29 loyalty program memberships per household. Of note, they found that only about 12 (less than half) were actually active in these programs.

Customer loyalty has become a catchphrase for what ultimately is the goal of most marketing strategies today. It is referred to as CRM, Customer Relationship Marketing, and what they are all trying to accomplish is the opportunity to increase customer loyalty. Just as each click on your Web site indicates a customer's willingness to try and stay engaged with you, so too does their multiple visits to your physical location. Customer loyalty is not the program but rather the end result of successful marketing combined with the customer's experiences over time.

Have you ever pondered why they put the milk in the back of the supermarket, about as far away from the entrance as possible? These operators are hopeful that their customers pass the many thousands of items on their way to the land of milk and cheese. Shopping behaviorist Herb Sorensen disagrees with that strategy. He accurately suggests it causes shoppers emotional distress and they will simply purchase their milk elsewhere. As a result of failing to understand how their customers act in their stores, these supermarkets lose billions of dollars each year. It's not these billions that are troublesome—rather, it's the opportunity for another retailer to convert what may have been a loyal customer into a defector.

In the latest US Grocery Shopper Trends report, it showed over 50 percent of all shopping trips are for five items or fewer, nearly 16 percent are for just one item. Quick-trip shoppers are a major segment most retailers ignore as they focus more of their efforts on stock-up shoppers. This customer is screaming for convenience and, to no surprise, this quick-trip shopper is now considered a major segment in the shopping industry. As a result, you have seen convenience stores like Kwik Trip and Aldi emerging to fill this profitable gap. Why in the world would you give the customer a reason to shop elsewhere? If you are, it's a broken model and you should address it—fast.

In the early days of car sharing, it was normal to go to a physical location to pick up your keys and then another location to pick up your car. Zipcar changed that broken model of logic across the globe by removing this unnecessary stop at the key depot. Every driver can simply download the app on their mobile device and get their car.

The key to a successful customer-driven organization is the acquisition and maintenance of customers. You need both, but putting too much focus on the acquisition basket is both expensive and not wise. Zappos, the shoe retailer, has it right as they earn close to 75 percent of their sales from repeat customers. The repeat customers are rewarded and spend 25 percent more than first-time buyers. They even give their customers up to one year to return an item and there are never any hidden charges. In fact, if you purchase on 2/29 of a leap year, then you have until 2/29 the following leap year to return those orders. That's four whole years! The Zappos experience is fun and easy.

Steal market share from the other guys and above all else take care of the customers you have. It is proven that some of the most successful businesses see up to 80 percent of their revenue come from just 20 percent of their customers. Neglecting this customer base in the pursuit of attracting new customers can be an expensive and flawed approach.

A significant opportunity in this arena exists at car dealerships all over the country. Dealerships are spending on average at least $400 per car sold on advertising—whether it's direct mail, e-mail, TV, or the Internet—just to bring more customers in. Even more dealerships are paying additional dollars on social and mobile marketing that only adds to the per-car expense. What amazes me is that there is very little connection between the sales advertising side and the service area side. Think about it, they have customers coming in every day who have manufacturer's warranties that are expiring, have possibly locked into a higher interest rate, or have enough equity in their current car that can be used to put a down payment on a new one. There is no added expense getting these customers in.

Now the answer is not to put a salesperson in the service area. I have seen that before and it failed miserably—namely because they approached selling cars in the service area the same way they did in the showroom. High energy and going for the close in the service area was not going to drive new car sales and actually turned off customers. Rather, you have to make it about improving the customers' experience. While you are reviewing their needs during the service appointment, you are also letting them know about the best available options that bring value to the relationship. That is connecting with the customer.

Here is a recent example where a company was disconnected from me—their once loyal customer. Living in Milwaukee, I was a very frequent flyer of Midwest Airlines before they were bought out by Frontier. This airline provided me with a service of more direct flights than their competition, early boarding, bonus miles, and above average service. In 2009, Air Tran came to town and offered better pricing, equal service, and the same bonus miles I was getting with Midwest Airlines.

Now the executives at Midwest on paper probably considered me a very loyal customer . . . and I was. I would guess their metrics relied on satisfaction and loyalty analysis as tools to validate this. The problem is these metrics only focus on past and present. Satisfaction and loyalty are extremely time sensitive and a look down the road approach is essential. With Air Tran offering all that Midwest did but at a more attractive price, my loyalty changed instantly and I have never looked back. If Midwest would have been more proactive (that 20 percent I mentioned earlier), delivered a better service experience than their competition, and stayed in touch with their best customers, they may have kept me. More contact is a good thing. In fact, a Bain & Company study found that 67 percent of existing customers "go elsewhere because no one stays in touch with them." Loyalty today is fleeting. A customer only needs a reason, however slight, to go elsewhere. Don't give them one or at least give them many more reasons to stay.

Let me give you a couple of numbers to support why customer satisfaction and retention makes smart business.

- *It costs 10–20 times more to recruit a new customer than it does to keep an existing one.*

- *A customer loyalty gain of 5 percent can raise lifetime profits per customer as much as 95 percent.*

- *An increase in loyalty of just 2 percent has been proven to equate to a 10 percent cost reduction in some sectors.*

Why are loyal customers so important? Because they purchase your products and services again and again over time. Disney has devised ways to tap into their loyal customers and greatly expand their market share. They built hotels and cruise ships so guests would spend more time on company properties. Coincidently, they also brand these venues at every possible opportunity. I have even had some of my conference attendees tell me this branding impacted their future vacation planning as their kids helped drive the decision for next year's vacation. It's never too early to start building your loyal customers. If you give them a reason, this group is more likely to stay with you when your competition opens up down the street or online.

✿ More Likely to Stick with You When a Service Blunder or Event Occurs

The Chinese character for the word "crisis" consists of two separate symbols, one signifying danger and the other signifying opportunity. When you miss a step, screw-up, disappoint a customer—call it what you want—your service recovery opportunity is far easier with a customer that you have built a relationship with. Customer loyalty is akin to them sticking with you in tough economic times. If you are forced to raise prices, they remain committed because you gave them other reasons to stay. Even if they are thinking about switching, they will committedly give you the benefit of the doubt before doing so.

When Taco Bell was sued by a law firm alleging it misled the public about the contents of its taco meat, the management reached out to their most loyal customers via the fast-food chain's Facebook page. They quickly seized the moment and announced it would give away 10 million tacos to members who "like" their Facebook page. In less than a week, Taco Bell had 5 million followers who liked its Facebook page. CEO Greg Creed said, "We found it only fitting to reward these 5.4 million fans and a friend with a free taco. It's our way of saying thanks for their loyalty and support."

Retailers that create these emotional ties with their customers realize that the value of their customers is determined over all of their purchases—not just with a single one. They also have learned that their best customers are not always the ones that make the biggest purchases but rather those that come back repeatedly.

❧ *More Likely to Refer Your Products and Services to Others*

Your loyal customers are the best evangelists you have. Referrals from trusted friends, neighbors, and their social network groups remain one of the least expensive yet powerful marketing messages for your organization. This group feels an intrinsic attachment to your product and service and wants to tell others. They don't just recommend you to friends, but do so passionately. If customer defection is the silent killer, these are your raving fans.

Zappos is a great example of a company that celebrates both internal and external customer loyalty. Through a campaign featuring puppet-like characters based on actual employees, they successfully demonstrated to existing and new customers how the online retailer's employees made the process of ordering or even returning products easy. "The goal is that when you see the ads, in TV, print or digital, you'll say, 'That's the Zappos I know,' or, 'That's a company I want to do business with,'" said Aaron Magness of Zappos.

Recently, my wife and I stopped at our favorite local restaurant, which is Bacchus in downtown Milwaukee. We arrived early coming from a sporting event and were delighted to see that their staff members were taking a moment to sit down and eat dinner. Turns out this is something they do before every shift, which gives them the opportunity to come together as a family. This bonding time consists of not only the wait staff but also the hosts, dishwashers, managers, and chefs. My crystal ball is in the shop for an oil change, but I would guess their employee retention is tops in the industry. After this wonderful meal, how do you think the employees treat their customers? Bacchus has a very loyal following including my family. It's no surprise that this business recognizes their loyal employees and customers who in turn recognize them right back.

Is Customer Loyalty Behavioral, Attitudinal, or Both?

Let's start by acknowledging that loyalty is not just given with a card. Customer loyalty has long been viewed as being behavioral or attitudinal. The behavioral approach suggests that customers remain loyal as long as they continue to buy your goods or services. Some maintain that the strongest evidence of loyalty under this model represents the percentage of those customers who were likely to recommend you to a friend. I maintain that the customer's intent to shop your business again is a higher indicator of loyalty but both are very strong measures.

The attitudinal approach maintains that customers feel a sense of attachment, trust, or commitment to the product or service. You gave them multiple reasons to stay attracted to your business. Followers of Apple and Starbucks exhibit an almost cult-like attitudinal approach to these businesses. Their approach to satisfaction is "What we do" and engagement as "How we do it." But these companies know that customers are only as loyal as their options and work to innovate continually.

Studying the best of the best, those businesses that maintain the highest loyalty rates in their respective industries, I have found they all have behavior and attitudinal advantages over their competition. It's the combination of these approaches that positions them, and ultimately you, as you look to drive higher loyalty conversion rates on a daily basis.

Are All Loyal Customers "Good"?

This is one of the most asked questions when doing Q & A after my seminars. It's kind of a slippery slope so I am always cautious when answering. In general, the most important thing is to keep focusing on your "right" customers. The majority of them will of course also be your most loyal customers. However, you may find a customer who takes up your resources, exhausts your staff, and never materially spends what you are expecting.

For example, I had a customer who would come into one of my stores almost on a daily basis. By all accounts, she was one of our most loyal customers. Even though she was elderly, she would insist on shopping by herself. On many occasions, however, she would spend hours walking around talking with associates and having them run back & forth to the stockroom, only to find out she never really wanted the items they retrieved. The associates would become so agitated each time this customer came in that she changed the morale of the entire store on those days.

Worse than that, this customer never talked kindly about the store or of the personal service she received. She had a terrorist mentality of her experience and nothing the associates or I could do was good enough. Her purchases were small to nonexistent, and what she did purchase was usually returned the following day.

In the end, I finally told her that we could no longer provide her the personal service she enjoyed even if that meant we lost her as a customer. A few weeks later, we never saw her again. You could see how much more energized the daytime staff was and how they were excited by the additional time they now had to spend with all of their loyal customers. Firing a customer can be as difficult as satisfying one. While it's best not to lose a customer, sometimes it is the right thing to do.

Would You Prefer Your Spouse to Be Satisfied or Loyal?

Guessing most of you said "loyal" and you're correct. That's why a satisfied customer is worthless as it relates to loyalty. Average equals satisfied and satisfied means nothing. Satisfaction tells you how your customer thinks you're doing as compared to loyalty, which tells you how they will spend their money. A customer can be satisfied with you but more satisfied with your competitor. It's like winning a lottery ticket but not cashing it in—it doesn't count.

Yankelovich Partners reported that 69 percent of consumers are interested in "products and services that would help them skip or block marketing." So trying to push loyalty on consumers is just not going to work. If you are reading this book, I would guess your business is working hard to build your brand image and that of the goods and services you sell. As we started out this chapter talking about marketing, these processes—such as advertising, targeting, and building loyalty programs—all attempt to create a long-term partnership. In the end, it will hopefully deliver repeat purchases and ultimately a more loyal customer. But more important than these initiatives are the daily executions of great customer service and thus satisfaction. When satisfaction goes up, so too follows loyalty.

Customer Satisfaction Does Not Necessarily Equate to a Correlation between Loyalty and Advocacy

If a customer gives you a high rating on satisfaction, but fails to advocate you to others or is not loyal to you, how do you react to that feedback? The Customer Satisfaction Score (CSAT) does not prove that satisfied customers are also loyal and want to give referrals. In fact, studies show approximately

40 percent of satisfied customers don't come back to a business. While this could be debated, I have always found that a customer who rates their CSAT as a 10 out of 10 will usually demonstrate actual loyalty that is a step or two lower on the ladder. Before you ask the question, very rarely have I seen the reverse. And if they rated you an 8 out of 10 (that feels ok, right?), new data suggests that 50 percent of this group had some sort of complaint. Keep going and nearly everyone that rated you a 6 out of 10 had a complaint. So if you think a 5 or 6 is a neutral score, think again.

My colleague Paula Courtney is the CEO of The Verde Group and an expert in the customer experience space. In a column, she addressed the question of whether high Net Promoter Scores (NPS) equated to high performance. Specifically, she stated, "That would be like watching videos of musicians with lots of tattoos and insisting their success was caused by the tattoos. You wouldn't make that leap. You'd know that the tattoos were a common feature of the musicians, but not the cause of their talent or popularity. Similarly, high Net Promoter Scores are a common feature of growing companies, but not necessarily the cause of their success."

There is very little relationship between the customer's perception of a transaction and loyalty. To take it a step further, I would also suggest you don't directly connect loyalty (which is an emotional tie) and advocacy (a willingness to speak on behalf of someone other than themselves). Instead, research has shown very clearly that multiple very satisfying experiences are needed to boost a customer's loyalty level.

For example, you might have a customer who rates their interactions with a business very high. Let's say the customer gives you over 90 percent on each of his or her past several visits that gives you a really high CSAT score. But the customer then decides to leave and you are left scratching your head. When you finally drill down into the issues, it turns out the customer actually reported the same problem affecting him five times in a row. He may have been pleased that your support fixed it each time, but had to be unhappy with the product, in general, for having that continued problem.

I spend a lot of my time shopping retailers and in many instances am offered an opportunity to take a survey as part of my transaction. Some would argue that surveying has gotten out of hand. Seems any time you fly, shop, bank, call customer service, visit a doctor, or go out to eat, they are asking you to take a survey. While in-store or online measurement surveys can be helpful inputs and businesses can learn from these, it represents only a single view of the customer experience. It is critical to capture all relative data via all relevant milestones of the customer's journey with the brand. If you are asked to invest in a start-up or new venture opportunity, I am guessing you wouldn't base your decision on a single metric. Like the annual physical assessment, my doctor does a battery of tests. You wouldn't trust a doctor who measured your health by only checking your blood pressure.

So too should your feedback come from review sites, comment cards, the call center, and even associate feedback.

Social measurement is just starting to gain ground on the traditional survey because they can now provide a score and better measure your brand through data analytics. Speaking of social, according to a study by VentureBeat, social media users complain 879 million times a year on Facebook, Twitter, and other social media platforms.

Whether customers are complaining because their foot-long Subway sandwich is only 11 inches or tweeting about "the rudest agent in Denver" when the agent wouldn't let his two elementary school-age children board the plane early with him. Did you hear about that one? It turns out they kicked him and his two kids off the flight until he agreed to delete the tweet. Complaints via social media are growing fast—real fast—as it's proven that customers are more satisfied complaining via a social platform than doing so in a traditional manner. The other significant advantage is the closer we can get to the customer by seeking their feedback in these moments of truth, the more accurate their feelings and feedback will be. In fact, 40 percent more accurate than feedback collected just 24 hours earlier, according to Gartner.

The goal is to provide a 360-degree view of the customer experience across all of these platforms and pulse out trends that you collect from the feedback. For example, I am seeing traditional call centers focus much less on metrics like average handle time—which is how long someone is on the phone—because it doesn't equate directly to the quality of the experience and it doesn't speak to whether the customer is satisfied or, more importantly, highly satisfied. They will stay involved with these metrics but they won't be front and center in associate conversations.

Speaking of call centers, an extreme example of this new thinking comes from Delta Airlines. I phoned Delta to change a flight and, when prompted, agreed to take a survey after my call with the representative was completed. The Delta representative could not have been more accommodating, helpful, and empowered to get me on a flight I needed to be on but probably didn't deserve. When he disconnected, I got transferred to take the survey. A one-question survey. I repeat, a ONE-question survey, which asked me to simply answer on a 1-5 scale the following question:

Based on your interaction with our agent, how likely would you be to hire them as a customer-service representative for your business?

How about that? I even liked Delta more after that call because I felt they respected my time. Clearly, they made the decision that asking that single question brought enough insight to make the survey response beneficial to the business. Needless to say, he got a five. And I certainly would.

Hey, Can I Have a 10?

If you are one of those businesses that say, "Give us a 10 because it's important to us" ("We don't really care if you're happy, we just care if we get high marks . . .") then your CSAT score is meaningless. For example, I have a choice of two Cadillac dealerships—both within 15 miles of our home—

that can service my vehicle. At one of the two dealers, the service manager approached and offered me a free oil change if I would rate them a 10 on the survey that would be coming out from General Motors. I politely declined and have never been back since. At a grocery store I visited, they had on the front of their associate shirts "My Goal Is Highly Satisfied Customers." Really, that's how your going to get highly satisfied customers? At another business, I witnessed associates with T-shirts that read as follows:

- *8's are not great!*

- *9's are not fine!*

- *Give us a 10!*

The aim of surveys is to make sure that we get results that can be translated into action that can benefit your customers, partners, and associates. This feedback can provide early warning signs for developing issues with customer facing services. It's not a focus on complaint reduction.

While attending a conference, I got involved in a discussion at the bar with several other attendees, one of whom mentioned she improved their customer experience score 40 percent this past year. Stunned, I asked her how she did that, and she shared that their accounting practices were very shabby and many of the invoices they sent out were just inaccurate. So they corrected that and only a few go out wrong anymore. Now ask yourself, would you ever be more loyal to this business or more importantly spend more because they offered you an accurate invoice? You don't need a complaint reduction strategy. You just need to reduce the problems you cause that generate the complaint.

That Cadillac dealer thought the numbers were the goal and that thinking will never let them leverage and integrate feedback that will make a difference. Instead of offering me a free oil change, his time would have been better spent simply talking with his customers, visiting the customer lounge, or engaging his previous day's customers with a follow-up phone call.

10

So Much Training, So Little to Show for It

"The Mediocre Teacher Tells.
The Good Teacher Explains.
The Superior Teacher Demonstrates.
The Great Teacher Inspires."
                                    William Arthur Ward

"Floss only the teeth you want to keep."
                                    Zig Ziglar

Consistent data, year after year, shows that the highest employee turnover rates are associated with those companies delivering the poorest service quality. There are countless books on associate engagement and turnover so I won't speak to those efforts. Operational challenges with the growing number of processes are now matched only by the growing number of technologies to support them. Training associates who turn over every 6–12 months has become an operational stumbling block. The key is to provide the right training before they interact with customers, and provide it in an easygoing manner where they can engage customers quickly and effectively.

When providing training, especially when a new associate starts, it's important to remember that they can't be engaged if they are overwhelmed. How many strategies, plans, and procedures can they focus on? Below are recommendations that will serve as a guide as you build your training program.

Walk the journey

A truly effective customer-training program identifies all of the touchpoints of the customer's journey and each of the interaction points where those two can intersect. Training for these touchpoints gets associates prepared, confident, and comfortable with the customer experience before they even hit the sales floor. Imagine the theatre manager building an exquisite set, promoting the performance, sewing amazing costumes but not taking the time to rehearse the actors. Companies do this every day when they turn the lights on, staff the store, and guide the teams to deliver great service but don't bother to properly prepare the staff.

Be, act, and think like a customer

If an associate is going to deliver excellent service, they will need to walk in the customer's shoes to understand what that looks like. When they do this, the real unlock will happen when they begin to anticipate a customer's needs in advance. I witnessed a hotel worker in a lobby standing outside the front desk. He noticed a guest coming in from the adjacent pool area. She had kids in tow, was wet, covered in towels, and was struggling to open the door to the lobby. When he saw her fumbling with the door latch, he came over and assisted her. That's good service, and if demonstrated in a training session, it would probably be given proper credit. But what if that hotel worker had assisted the guest immediately when he first saw her coming and realized she may struggle when she got to the door? Then instead of providing "reactive service," which corrects a negative experience, he would provide "anticipatory service," which prevents the negative experience from happening in the first place.

Train to look for the little things

There's a saying, "Enjoy the little things in life, because when you look back, those were the big things." When you train to see and deliver on the little things, most everything else will follow. This is definitely true and was witnessed firsthand on a skiing trip with our family and friends to Vail where Vail Resorts operates the facility. Their associates are trained to spot the little things. When one of the people in our group had a challenging time on the slopes, they offered him a free group ski lesson. They also put RFID technology into their passes so guests wouldn't have to fumble around and take off their gloves to show their lift ticket when it was scanned. With all that data they had collected, they went on to create a social game with an idea called EpicMix, an app that allows Vail Resort guests to share their vacation experiences via social media. The response was off the charts. Nearly 100,000 guests activated their EpicMix accounts and 45 percent of them shared their results on Facebook and Twitter. Darren Jacoby, Director of CRM for Vail Resorts, summarized it this way, "We had almost 2 million social posts this year, and over half of those included a photo. If you take Facebook's average of 130 friends in your network, that's potentially 260 million impressions. Those are all people talking about our brand and sharing their experience about that brand with their family and friends. Vail Resorts' mission is creating an experience of a lifetime. And we have an internal mantra underneath that experience of a lifetime of owning it, personalizing it, and elevating it. Our frontline associates do that every single day with our guests." And it all starts with the little things.

Train to care for the cold, not the sneeze

They say if you think your only tool is a hammer, every problem starts to look like a nail. Do you recall the scene from the movie *Meet the Parents* where Greg is at the airport and it's empty except for him, the boarding agent at his gate, and some guy vacuuming in the background? Greg approaches with his ticket. He's in row 8, but the gate agent has just announced through the loudspeaker that she's boarding rows 9 and above. "Please step aside, sir," she says in a perky, but firm tone. "It's just one row, don't you think it's okay?" he asks. "Nope. We'll call your row momentarily," she replies, and then asks him, with more determination, to step aside. After a few painful minutes, the gate agent once again picks up the loudspeaker to thank the invisible crowd for waiting and to board all remaining rows. When Greg steps forward, this stickler for protocol smiles and says hello as though he had not just been wishing her a slow and painful death.

This gate attendant would rather stick to the procedure than make the customer happy. By going by the book, the gate attendant puts him in a bad mood. She could have easily just let him on the plane earlier, but chose not to. Training is the perfect place to teach our associates very early on that there is a gaping divide between operations-focused and customer-focused. Clearly the gate agent in this example was following the book. She would rather stick to the procedure (operations focused—the sneeze) than make the customer happy (customer focused—the cold).

Continued Training

I had an executive at a conference tell me, "Annual customer-service training is like deodorant, within time it wears off and the odor comes back." I'm guessing an internal and ongoing service culture was not prevalent at his business. Training doesn't just stop when orientation is completed. This is about getting better and better.

"We can hire nice people and teach them to sell, but we can't hire salespeople and teach them to be nice."
Bruce Nordstrom

For many years, new employees at Nordstrom's were given a copy of the famous Nordstrom Employee "Handbook." A single 5 by 8 inch card containing just 75 words:

Welcome to Nordstrom

We're glad to have you with our Company. Our number one goal is to provide outstanding customer service. Set both your personal and professional goals high. We have great confidence in your ability to achieve them.

Nordstrom Rules: Rule #1: Use best judgment in all situations. There will be no additional rules.

Please feel free to ask your department manager, store manager, or division general manager any question at any time.

Times have progressed and now Nordstrom's new-hire orientation provides the just mentioned card but also includes a handbook of other more detailed rules and regulations as the way Nordstrom's operates has changed. But the spirit of what they look for in associates and, more importantly, how they're training them continues to be simple and easy to execute. It still serves them well even today.

Nordstrom is famous for its associate-empowerment practices. One can just look at their store return policy. According to the retail giant, when it comes to items bought in their stores, their return policy is . . . well, not to have one. "We don't actually have a return policy for purchases made at Nordstrom stores or at Nordstrom.com," they state on their web site. "We handle returns on a case-by-case basis with the ultimate objective of satisfying the customer. We stand behind our goods and services and want customers to be satisfied with them. We'll always do our best to take care of customers—our philosophy is to deal with them fairly and reasonably; we hope they will be fair and reasonable with us as well."

In other words, Nordstrom leaves each and every return situation up to the associate, and fosters an environment where they can use their judgment and focus on satisfying the customer.

When the Worship Ends, the Service Begins

If you hired correctly, trained properly, recognize, celebrate, coach, and reward along the way, then you don't need to worry about the retention numbers I opened this chapter with. Your team won't be performing like a quarterback who is functional only while being protected in the pocket. Instead they will be able to scramble and improvise on their feet because you spent the time and effort to ensure they understood that's what it takes for your business to be successful.

Associates require maintenance and updates as much as machines do. Consider retraining as maintenance that will make a difference. If you bought a million dollar machine, you wouldn't use it continuously without inspections, maintenance, or upgrades. Of course you wouldn't. Training is not an event. It's a continuous, lifelong process, necessary for the health of both your business and your associates. It's also not an expense. Paying expenses keeps the doors open, but investing in associate training opens new doors. Training development is an investment.

Lastly, training builds morale. Investing in your associates often demonstrates they have a future with the organization and you care. To build a team of loyal, fully engaged high achievers, hire the right people then invest in their training regularly.

11

Promise a Lot, But Deliver More— Meet Some Service All-Stars

"Being on par in terms of price and quality only gets you into the game. Service wins the game."

Tony Alessandra

"Your web site isn't the center of your universe. Your Facebook page isn't the center of your universe. Your mobile app isn't the center of your universe. The customer is the center of your universe."

Bruce Ernst

By now, I am guessing you will walk away understanding the universal truth that a brand is not what a company says it is, but what the customer feels it is. Studying the best service companies is one thing. Experiencing them is another. Arthur Blank, one of the founders of Home Depot, stated: "Nobody loves a company. A company is just a sign. Nobody loves brick and mortar. We are in the relationship business, not the transaction business."

What follows are my personal encounters with some of the best service providers out there today. Many of these companies you will read about are also found on published lists including *Business Week*, Forrester, and J.D. Power & Associates, which speaks to the consistency of these service providers.

The one constant that each of these organizations have embedded in their DNA is the connection between satisfied employees and evangelistic customers. Not just limited to the frontline but also living throughout the entire organization. They don't have a silver bullet, no single idea that innovates the customer journey. Instead, they harness the customer experience that drives above normal performance.

New research offers an update to our existing thinking of the service-profit chain, which links the front-liner to customer satisfaction. It stresses the importance of the "empathy engine," which analyzes the role of the entire organization including all levels of management. If we think of that engine as the heartbeat of the organization, the entire business has to pump the customer through it. It starts at the beginning, with how they organize themselves and how they place value on being obsessed about the customer. This empathetic approach will be noticeable as you read through the list of all-stars and should be a top-down/bottom-up focus of any business.

Another noticeable trait of these organizations is their desire to continually improve. Several that I have noted are considered to be industry leaders in customer service best practices. What is cool to experience and witness are the innovative approaches they take to becoming even better and solidifying their place at the top of their industry.

The Economics of Customer Excellence

Bain & Company analysis shows that companies that excel in the customer experience grow revenues 4 percent–8 percent above their market competitors. Namely because superior experience helps earn greater loyalty among customers, turning them into active promoters who tend to stay longer and buy more. As a result, these promoters have a lifetime value that can reach 6 to14 times that of detractors. Delivering a great experience that keeps promoters comes at a time when loyalty in many industries continues to erode. Bain & Company's research showed that two-thirds of the 1,208 senior executives they surveyed reported that customer loyalty has declined.

The best study I have seen linking service excellence to financial results comes from the Customer Experience Excellence Centre. They began the study by trying to understand international customer best practices. They did that over six years of ongoing research, across three continents with over 1 million customer evaluations touching over 900+ cross sector brands. They analyzed these interactions through the Six Pillars™ of customer experience excellence:

- **Personalization**—*using individualized attention to drive an emotional connection.*

- **Expectations**—*managing, meeting, and exceeding customer expectations.*

- **Time and Effort**—*minimizing customer effort and creating frictionless processes.*

- **Integrity**—*being trustworthy and engendering trust.*

- **Resolution**—*turning a poor experience into a great one.*

- **Empathy**—*achieving an understanding of the customer's circumstances to drive deep rapport.*

They proved that the Six Pillars are not simply predictors of customer experience success, but also of long-term financial value. They contrasted the top 100 performing brands in their survey to the FTSE 100 (a share index of the 100 companies listed on the London Stock Exchange with the highest market cap). Over a five-year period, the top 100 brands had achieved double the revenue growth of the FTSE 100—an average of 11 percent. They also showed a significant insulation from recessionary downturns in profitability compared to the other group. This perhaps is the clearest indicator yet that there is a direct association between customer service excellence and financial success.

The all-stars are not listed in any particular order and include publicly held, private, and family companies. Each company on the list is there because it earned my trust, whether through an isolated engagement or throughout multiple encounters. While I am sure some of you will debate the list—I get it, no worries. I too hope you have your own list and very much look forward to hearing from you. Simply go to my web site BrianDennisSpeaker.com and share your service heroes.

OK, here we go . . .

USAA

My wife, who was in the Navy for 24 years, is a member of USAA (United Services Automobile Association, a diversified financial services group offering banking, investing, and insurance to people and families that serve, or have served, in the United States military.)

When Pam was deployed to Landstuhl, Germany, they made our banking across 4,000 miles an almost seamless experience. She often touts USAA as a leader in the field of innovative service. With over 11 million members, 92 percent say they plan to stay for life and with a 97 percent member satisfaction rate, they are tops in their industry.

What makes USAA unique is that it delivers innovative service even while many of their members are located in distant places throughout the world. They continue to be listed among the top award winners in multiple categories and it's easy to see why. Our experience has always been positive, friendly, and educational. So what makes USAA so innovative and customer-driven—let's see . . .

- *They were the first bank to offer iPhone Deposits. When a member wants to deposit a check, they don't have to use an ATM or bank teller, rather they just take a picture of the check via an iPhone app and in a few minutes the money is in their account.*

- *They routinely text balances to soldiers in the field.*

- *They deeply discount members' car insurance when they are overseas.*

- *New reps attend sessions where they get the unique experience of dining on MRE's (meals ready to eat), which the troops consume while in the field. Each rep is even handed a real deployment letter (names are changed) that gets them thinking about the financial decisions their members will be facing and the emotions surrounding such an event. When we were notified that my wife would be deployed for 13 months, I really appreciated the reassuring voice on the other end at USAA.*

- *Call center agents receive bonuses. Earlier we talked about satisfied associates are better positioned to deliver better service, which leads to greater satisfaction and ultimately improved loyalty.*

- *Agents are not rushed through calls. Member satisfaction trumps every other measurable metric at the call center.*

- *Agents can utilize intelligent software that shows a history of the online screens the customers have viewed on the USAA site, which allows them to better anticipate questions. They can also track agent suggestions for customer friendly ideas.*

- *More than a million of their members have already registered for fingerprint authentication to securely log on to the USAA Mobile App.*

> ☙ *Social Media Strategy. This strategy was*
> *represented by 4 pillars of focus: listening,*
> *engaging, strengthening relationships, and*
> *innovation. As a result of listening and*
> *engaging, USAA was one of the first to offer*
> *ratings and reviews to their customers.*
> *Thousands of members have provided valuable*
> *reviews, and they in turn have capitalized*
> *on them to drive service and web site*
> *improvements.*

Marriott Hotels and Resorts

Like some of you, I have the opportunity to spend way too many nights at numerous name brand hotels every year. Many do a good job, most fail at keeping me loyal to a particular brand. Marriott is unique in that they understand their customer intimately across 30 brands and their best customers even more than that.

According to the company's Web site, the first of Marriott's core values is to put people first: "Take care of associates and they will take care of the customers."

Marriott consistently goes the extra mile. For example, I forgot to charge my iPhone during the day, and I asked the valet if he could look in my rental car for the charger. The man literally jumped to help me, and after determining there was no charger in the car, offered to buy me a car charger at the store down the street. I told him no worries as I could just grab one at the airport. About five minutes later, I get a knock at my door and there he is with a cord that he found in a box that a previous guest must have left in their room. What's impressive about Marriott is not just the valet that delivers excellent service.

Consistently, every department delivers that "wow" moment, no matter how small the task. It just doesn't happen on its own but rather is guided by leaders who live and breathe J. Willard Marriott's original goal for the business: "good food and good service at a fair price."

Nearly 3,000 of Marriott's managers began their careers in hourly positions. They rave about their workplace and they stick around. The average tenure for a hotel general manager at Marriott is 25 years. Marriott has been on the Best Companies to Work For list for each of the 18 years the list has been published. Only eleven other companies can say that. This background provides a greater understanding of the customer that cannot be gained from a training manual or orientation. It also details why Marriott has one of the highest retention rates in the industry.

They are not resting on their laurels either, as they are passionately reinventing themselves to the next generation of travelers. Those new travelers—namely millennials—don't use drawers, like their closets without doors, and seldom use the desk and chair. Rather, they prefer to use their laptop or iPad from the bed. Marriott is adjusting a new room configuration to meet these needs.

The Marriott slogan, "Success is never final," has never been better demonstrated than at a two-day event that I attended at the Marriott World in Orlando, Florida. While I could praise so many wonderful individuals at this resort that made this meeting a success, one in particular defined the essence of what any organization would want in an associate. That individual is Mark Beaupre, Director of Food/Beverage and Executive Chef. Mark has since been promoted to the Director of Food/Beverage at the Gaylord Texan—another signature Marriott property.

Like many of you, I have had the privilege of meeting some great customer-service providers in my lifetime. I have even met a few who lived and breathed the customer experience where it translated into their lives at work and beyond. However, very rarely have I ever met a person as unique and gifted as he. Mark is in fact a "brand" in himself that surpassed any expectation I had of food, presentation, service, partnership, and team.

With a very limited budget, Mark created an event for the numerous volunteers that replicated the finest meals and beverages you would find anywhere. When the attendees checked in, many of them travelling over 6 hours to get there, Mark anticipated their long day and had complimentary appetizers and fresh squeezed lemonade available. His team created small touches throughout the resort that were noticeable by the attendees at the conference.

While I have called out one individual here, there are many Mark Beaupre's in the Marriott organization. Many that I have been privileged to know and to be served by, which have created lasting relationships.

Domino's

I thought this one might surprise you. I didn't put this company on my list because if I want to order a pizza and get it quick, there is no one faster. I didn't put them on my list because they are my favorite pizza—hey, I am a Chicago guy, what can I say? Rather, they are on my list because they really aren't a pizza company at all anymore. They are an e-commerce/technology company that happens to sell pizza and is incredibly dialed in on the customer-ordering experience. In fact, at the company's headquarters in Ann Arbor, Michigan, a third of Domino's total employees are dedicated to tech and digital platforms.

Domino's has been the leader of pizza-ordering technology for several years now but are continually improving upon that experience. They offer the customer numerous ways to order their pizza:

- *Good old-fashioned phone call*

- *A visit to their web site*

- *Via the Pebble or Android Wear smartwatch apps*

- *Through your Samsung Smart TV*

- *By Twitter by tweeting #EASYORDER.*
  Via text, by simply texting the pizza emoji or
  "EASYORDER" to DPIZZA, hungry customers

*who have previously set up a personal pizza
profile and added their mobile number can put
in their order.*

"There are an estimated eight trillion texts sent every year worldwide," says Patrick Doyle, president and CEO of Domino's. "With so many people using their devices to generally communicate in this way, it made sense to allow our customers the chance to order pizza that way, too."

They even let customers watch the progress of their order online in real time via Domino's pizza tracker, which shows you exactly when your order is put in the oven and sent out for delivery. It's easy to see why Domino's is the market-share leader in the delivery segment and has the second-largest share in the carryout segment.

Heal App

After giving a keynote speech at the San Diego Convention Center, I returned to my nearby hotel room soon after as I didn't feel very well. I immediately called down to the front desk to get some tea delivered and asked them to follow up with a wake-up call as I had a flight home later that evening. When the call came, I was feeling much worse and inquired if there was an in-house doctor or clinic nearby. The young lady on the phone directed me to an app called Heal. The app offers the equivalent of a modern day house call by the doctor. It's very much like the ride-hailing app Uber, but rather than a driver, they dispatch a family practice doctor and even send notifications as they approach your home, business, or hotel. Everything your primary doctor can do, so can they. The company has some in-network relationships with Anthem Blue Cross of California and Blue Cross Blue Shield of California. But since I was traveling and these are not in my network, I was charged a flat $99 for the visit. Technology and health care converging to deliver a customer experience that you thought was extinct years ago. All checked out okay—seems I might have had an allergic reaction to some food I had for lunch and was able to make my flight home that evening.

Lush

Ranked #1 out of 272 brands in the UK Customer Champion study, Lush sets the standard for customers. There may be no other company that is as transparent as they are. Lush is a cosmetics company that sells amazing products, has incredible ethics, and employs really fun people. Lush Kitchen allows you to view and follow your product as it is being made. They continually change their menu with an endless offering of new and improved product lines. When my wife and I walked into their store in Chicago for the first time, I can only equate her actions to that of a kid in a candy store. Their merchandise is made only from fresh, natural ingredients and it's easy to see why Lush is rapidly taking the beauty scene by storm. With products ranging from the ever so popular bath bombs to facial cleansers and solid shampoo to moisturizers, these eclectic and handmade toiletries are 100 percent vegetarian.

Many of Lush's cosmetics are unpackaged to avoid creating unnecessary waste. For the small selection of products that are packaged, the plastic is 100 percent recycled! They also have a hand and body lotion called Charity Pot. One hundred percent of the proceeds from this sweet smelling lotion go to the store's "Charity Pot Fund," which provides to environmental, humanitarian and animal rights charities. Lush has garnered a lot of attention for their strict policy regarding the testing of their products, taking a firm stance against animal testing by only utilizing human volunteers.

While all of that is great, what really sets Lush apart is their frontline employees. Lush gives their team the freedom to make in-the-moment decisions and go off-script when warranted if they feel it's the right thing to do for the customer. Their empowered employees take great pride and ownership in their jobs when they know they can exercise independent judgment to satisfy a customer.

Trader Joe's

Why is it Trader Joe's sells twice as much per square foot as Whole Foods? Because Trader Joe's knows its audience. They are passionately focused on product innovation and selling groceries and wine at cheap prices. Because customers know they can get high-quality stuff at a low price, they are incredibly loyal to Trader Joe's.

Eighty percent of Trader Joe's products are in-house, meaning that customers can't get them anywhere else and the grocer can sell them at lower prices. They sell lots of random but excellent products that you didn't know existed but end up buying. I never thought I would need potato chips dipped in chocolate or goats milk Brie cheese, but somehow they always make it into my basket.

They deliver on the little things like atmosphere and incredibly fast checkouts along with courteous cashiers. Oh yeah, and they are in Hawaiian shirts because, as Trader Joe puts it, "we're traders on the culinary seas, searching the world over for cool items to bring home to our customers. And when we return home, we think grocery shopping should be fun, not another chore."

When shopping in their downtown Chicago location, I asked one of their crew members where the cookie butter was. She asked me if I had ever tried cookie butter, to which I responded, "No." She then took me directly to it in the aisle, proceeded to open the jar, and then handed me a plastic spoon to try it.

And that charming bell sound you hear while you're there. The bells are a kind of Trader Joe's Morse code. Those blustery PA systems just didn't feel right to them, so they came up with a simple system to communicate. One bell lets their Crew know when to open another register. Two bells means there are additional questions that need to be answered at the checkout. Three bells calls a manager-type person over to checkout.

One irony of Trader Joe's that speaks to its entrenched in-store customer culture is their 1-800 number that only provides customers with a voice recording of store locations. Now, that does not appear to be a trait of a service all-star, does it? But if you look closer, you'll see that they take the approach that listening to their customers' really valuable feedback is not about taking concerns to a call center. Instead, the leaders believe in direct interaction at store level where any and all concerns can be addressed to their guests' satisfaction. Instead of reacting to the customers' feedback via a phone call, they want to effectively respond to it immediately in the store.

12

So, Now What?

There is a story of a wealthy man who called his servant and told him he was leaving the country for a year and that while he was gone, he wanted the servant to build him a house. The wealthy man told him to build it well, and when he returned, he would pay all the bills for material and labor.

Shortly after the employer left, the servant decided that he was foolish to work so hard, so he started cutting corners and squandering the money he saved. When his master came back, he paid all the bills and then asked the servant, "Are you satisfied with the house?" When the servant said that he was, the master said, "Good . . . because the house is yours. You can live in it now the rest of your life."

And now I ask you, if your business is your house, are you building the kind of house that you will be proud to live in forever? Are you cutting corners that don't remove customer obstacles or squandering time, commitment, and effort? My guess is if you made it this far in the book, you're not like the servant, but it's a great lens to keep in front of us so as to never relax our standards.

Did you ever hear of the phrase "run to daylight"? Living in Wisconsin, it's almost required to read the book *RUN to Daylight* by the legendary football coach of the Green Bay Packers Vince Lombardi. The title refers to the Packers most famous play, "the Packers Sweep." When players executed the sweep correctly, defensive players couldn't stop it. In the play, the quarterback hands the football to the running back who runs laterally toward the sidelines but keeps the goal line in sight. The linemen do the same, but keep their eyes peeled for an opposing player to block. The running back's job is to pivot or change direction upfield once he sees "daylight between the linemen." The play illustrates the importance of preplanning and being prepared for the opportunities that arise and then quickly taking advantage of them. This is the thinking I want to leave you with. If you hire right, lead correctly, engage your associates, and stay focused on delivering a great customer experience, then you will be prepared to pivot when needed. More importantly, your associates can pivot on their own because they understand the vision and importance of your customer-centric lens. What's magical to witness is when they do it without even thinking—it just happens. They say great baseball players can tell when the ball hits the bat that it's going to be a home run. They don't have to see it; they feel it. The same is true of associates that understand the vision and are given the autonomy to deliver great service. A boss who micromanages is like a coach who wants to get in the game. Great service leaders guide and support . . . then sit back and cheer from the sidelines.

Research indicates that people in US stores buy more German wine when a store's sound system plays German music and more Italian wine when it plays Italian music. However, shoppers claim the background music has no effect on their wine choices. Great organizations go about delivering a service experience that at times may not be noticeable to the customer directly, but is so consistently repeated that it delivers a quiet yet elevated level of service. More and more customers expect the levels of customer satisfaction they receive from leaders such as Apple, Google, and Amazon, and they expect this from even the smallest businesses across many industries. With the advent of technology and how brands set industrial standards, the competition mentioned has scaled up to a point where customers are used to a certain level of expertise from service providers. Customers want to see, feel, and experience the unexpected, not the everyday.

Know Thy Customer

These organizations painstakingly get as close to their customers as possible. They know their customers inside and out. Ask any dentist when their biggest emergency day is, when visits surge, and they will tell you the day after St. Paddy's day. It's consistently about 60–80 percent higher than any other day in the year. Some people behave badly on that day, and they can predict it and plan for the increased workload. How about asking a big-box housewares retailer what day they sell the most wineglasses on every year? If they know their customer, they will tell you the Tuesday of Thanksgiving week. Why? Because that is when many Americans begin preparing their tableware for the big day and realize some of their previous glasses have broken or may have more guests attending.

When planning a recent vacation, I went online to a web site that we use frequently and purchased a camera. After doing so, I was curious what else they would offer me that might go along with my camera. Perhaps a long range zoom lens or rugged carrying case? I was eager to see what they would entice me with. You know, they tried to upsell me with another camera. I don't need another camera I just bought one—remember? If they knew their customer—I mean really knew their customer—they could offer relevant, niche exciting, and needed products that I just couldn't resist. Now, this is not an easy task. Amazon, for instance, introduces close to a half-million products on average each day. But for the retailers that can utilize next-generation data and analytics, it is an incredible opportunity to get closer to your customer and drive targeted sales.

Writer Richard Matheson tells the story of when a married couple is given a box by a mysterious stranger. On the box is a button and the stranger informs them that if they push it they will instantly receive $50,000, but somewhere in the world a person they did not know will die. They agonize for days over what to do. One day, the woman gives in and presses the button. Moments later, her husband is struck by a train and killed. Furious, she confronts the man who gave them the box and demands to know why it was her husband who dies. "Lady," the man replies, "Did you really think you knew your husband?"

A little melodramatic but underscores the greater point that there is a real danger in assuming you know your customer—when you don't. To deliver customer service excellence, you have to know your customer, research your customer, be your customer . . . whoever they are or may become.

There is an African proverb that says, "Every morning there is a lion who must get up early and run after his food. And every morning there is a deer who must get up early in order not to be someone's food." So whatever you do after reading this book, you better get running. You better get started because your mission is to find a way out of no way. Or someone else will.

Bonus

101 Tips, Tricks, and Other Thoughts about the Customer Experience to Ponder

1. *Customers do not see channels, they see experiences.*

2. *Write with the wrong hand to better understand your customer. Using your less dominant hand to manipulate a fork or to brush your teeth can be uncomfortable but affords a new opportunity to look at things. Challenge the status quo.*

3. *You can win at baseball and you can win at football, but you can't be playing both on the same field—understand who your customer is.*

4. *Every good idea was at one time an innovation—why not this one?*

5. *All within the organization must understand their part. If you veer off that course too far, it's like a big ship on the ocean. A tenth of a degree will get you in the wrong country.*

6. *Everyone, and I mean everyone, is a customer.*

7. *The best way to find out what a customer wants is to listen.*

8. *Don't roll up the red carpet after the customer purchases—this is the time to start unrolling it.*

9. *Profitability and market share don't suffer when you focus on "top box" customer satisfaction. Just the opposite happens: they improve.*

10. *Create fans and your customers will follow.*

11. *Collect data at every touchpoint and build a holistic picture of your customers' journey.*

12. *Customer service is the new PR.*

13. *And it doesn't end at 6 on Friday.*

14. *Focus on the right stuff. Never get bored with the basics—they are an important part of the experience.*

15. *Define standards with a customer-centric view.*

16. *Recognize your associates when they deliver great service—it's like free fuel.*

17. *Never underestimate the impact of associate engagement on your customer experience.*

18. *Numbers are not the goal—delivering great service is.*

19. *Feedback is a gift—complaint satisfaction is strongly correlated with increased brand loyalty.*

20. *Word of mouth from dissatisfied complainants is more than double the word of mouth communicated by satisfied complainants.*

21. *Don't signal right and turn left—when you say you want to put the customer first, be certain that your business execution follows this same road.*

22. *Measure what matters to your customers, not you.*

23. *The best view of the customer experience requires boots on the ground.*

24. *Be quick to take action on customer, associate, and market feedback.*

25. *What's the difference between a rut and a grave? One is just a little bit deeper.*

26. *Disrupt your industry. Porsche is an innovation company, not a car company. They used to support their help desk with mechanics, now they staff with IT associates.*

27. *Properly train your associates. That means arming them with the best tools and information that is available. Don't keep adding to a manual that's five years old.*

28. *Whether it is 30, 300 or 30,000—scale the experience without sacrifice.*

29. *Develop a deep understanding of what matters to your customers then action those findings into a set of simple principles or standards to guide behavior all the way down to the front line.*

30. *The road to failed customer experience programs is paved with good intentions.*

31. *Don't let someone else take care of your customers.*

32. *Reinvent customer journeys using digital technologies.*

33. *Create a common purpose with your customers at the center. At Disney, all of their cast members share an aspiration called the "Common purpose to 'create happiness'."*

34. *Customers want to feel like they are in control of their journey—so let them. Ritz-Carlton Hotels greets guests with a welcome e-mail before they arrive and a personalized welcome letter in the room.*

35. *It's difficult to hear a sound when you clap with one hand. Develop the team to deliver service excellence, and you'll have multiple hands clapping.*

36. *The pessimist complains about the wind. The optimist expects it to change. The realist adjusts the sails.*

37. *Spread the wealth. No single customer, including Amazon, makes up more than 3 percent of FedEx's total revenue. All your customers are important.*

38. *Your customer's perception is reality.*

39. *Customer vision without execution is like a plane without wings.*

40. *Customers who opt to stick their necks out for you become your best marketers.*

41. *A strong customer-service culture cannot be copied.*

42. *Customer success does not occur in a vacuum.*

43. *Don't be a service robot.*

44. *Teamwork can multiply your talent. In the movie Rocky, Rocky Balboa describes his romance with his girlfriend Adrian, "I've got gaps. She's got gaps. But together we've got no gaps." It illustrates that a team with different abilities can be effective.*

45. *T.S. Elliot said, "Anyone can carve a goose were it not for the bones". You'll have bones to carve around every day so build an associate base that can deliver when challenges come up.*

46. *Customers expect companies to share their burdens—that's why Amazon notifies you when you already purchased a title on your Kindle and why your local pharmacy reminds you it's time to refill that prescription. What*

used to be a customer's responsibility is now woven into the business framework of a great experience.

47. *Customer success is not about a few people having better answers; it's about everyone asking better questions.*

48. *Be your customer—walk in their shoes.*

49. *Make the service experience memorable—be part of someone's dinner conversation.*

50. *The customer in front of you ALWAYS takes precedence over the one on the phone.*

51. *First impressions matter.*

52. *Last impressions matter.*

53. *Lose the fine print.*

54. *Focus on the very first customer experience. It's like being on a first date. There is very little forgiveness if this experience is not a good one.*

55. *Add personality to responses on every channel—genuine engagement is welcomed by customers so forget the canned answer. It's no fun talking to a logo.*

56. *Don't lose a customer over a refund. If you want to emulate a return policy, take a look*

at The Fog Creek Promise: "If you're not satisfied, for any reason, within 90 days you get a full refund, period, no questions asked. We don't want your money if you're not amazingly happy."

57. *Appreciate the power of "yes."*

58. *The customer might not always be right, but they should almost always win.*

59. *Humanize your brand. Accenture data shows 83 percent of US consumers prefer dealing with human beings over digital channels to solve customer-service issues and get advice.*

60. *Be empathetic and share your own experiences whenever possible.*

61. *Always give more than expected.*

62. *Tell your customer every chance you have how much you appreciate their business.*

63. *Take it off social media. One-on-one dialog is many times the preferred route after a customer has gotten your attention. Then encourage the customer to go back on social to celebrate the outcome.*

64. *Never forget who your loyal customers are.*

65. *Your staff will treat customers the way they are treated.*

66. *Make sure your customers know where to turn when they are not being treated properly— make it easy to get up the chain of command when needed. Better yet, solve their problem well before it would need to go that far.*

67. *Make training continuous—not a one-time event.*

68. *Never make the customer work.*

69. *Continually innovate the customer experience—never stop improving.*

70. *Be visible. Your customers and associates will notice.*

71. *Some of your customers are grumpy and flat-out wrong—and that's ok.*

72. *The extra touch matters—go above and beyond.*

73. *Customers don't owe you a thing.*

74. *The customer isn't always right, but they are the customer.*

75. *Don't serve, give service. You'll know the difference.*

76. *Go ahead and make their day.*

77. *A customer is NOT a customer until the second time they buy from you. The first time they are just a trial user.*

78. *Yes first, how later.*

79. *Small gestures, big rewards. A restaurant we were in brought us some bruschetta to the table to sample before our meal. A little gesture that worked as I now order that appetizer every time I visit.*

80. *Make the customer the hero of your story.*

81. *Don't try to separate the product from the experience. That's like trying to separate a bark from the dog and selling the bark separately.*

82. *Avoid ever referring to policy when talking with your customers.*

83. *Remember the other 93 percent. Communication is only 7 percent verbal.*

84. *Good service makes a difference. Great service makes them loyal.*

85. *Take a lesson from Walt Disney: "Do what you do so well that they want to see it again & bring their friends."*

86. *Your brand is an asset that you own jointly with your customers—treat them as your partner in everything you do.*

87. *Engage your outspoken customers.*

88. *Take ownership when things go wrong.*

89. *If a customer thinks your company sucks, agree & sympathize with them. Then start to win them back.*

90. *Reviews are not your enemy. They're a valuable gift of free and timely feedback.*

91. *What if it were you with this problem? How would you want it handled?*

92. *Be the one to inspire.*

93. *You can't change the world one customer at a time by yourself—take the team with you.*

94. *Just as you can't expect nine women to make a baby in a month—your road to service greatness will not happen overnight. Take it one customer at a time.*

95. *The best service sometimes is no service. If a customer has a question, then ask yourself why that is.*

96. *Everyone wears the sheriff's badge.*

97. *Deliver consistency that creates confidence your customers will have in you each and every time.*

98. *Recognize your associates for delivering a great service experience—handwritten notes still go a long way.*

99. *If you're at a call center, let them hear you smile.*

100. *Thank your customers who complain—it shows they want to do business with you.*

101. *Have fun, life is too precious.*

Acknowledgments

To my wife and best friend, Pam, I want to thank you for your unwavering sacrifice to help make this book a reality. Never once have you complained about the hours, travel, and incredibly cluttered office that were part of this project. This journey with you has been filled with joy, laughter, love, and a kick to my ass when it was needed. I never met anyone who can leave a positive impact on another so quickly, whether it's a new acquaintance or commanding large groups as a Navy Captain. You truly make this world a better place.

   To my son, Brian, who will always be way smarter than his dad. I am humbled by your incredible work ethic and all that you have accomplished in your short life. But I am even prouder of your kindness and willingness to always help another person out. I remember when you were in 4th grade and the teacher was badgering a young girl in your class for an answer she clearly didn't know. You burst out, "For the love of God, she doesn't know the answer." When we got a call that evening from your instructor letting us know she didn't need any help teaching the class, I knew you were going to be a great leader.

To my daughter, Brianna, who has a laugh that could be heard for miles. Your eye and talent for fashion is an incredible skill that will serve you well as you begin your studies in that field. You have taught me so much about how the young generation thinks, acts, and buys.

To my sister, Michelle, the mother of triplets and a son, you have always been an inspiration to me, and I am in continual amazement of all that you accomplish. If they wrote a book on how to be a perfect mom, sister, and friend, you would certainly be on the cover.

To Karen Saunders, my book designer and mentor in the publishing world. Karen has more patience than anyone I have ever known and has stood by me from the day we met. Not only a talented publisher and expert around all things that go into the making of a book, she is a friend who I will always cherish.

About the Author

Brian is recognized inter-
nationally as an industry
expert and is a sought-out
and award-winning key-
note speaker, panelist, and
key contributor on the inte-
gration of "simplifying" the
customer experience. He
has spoken to and trained
attendees that represent
over 200 of the Fortune 500
companies in 11 countries.

Brian serves on the advisory board for Nextpoint and
serves on the board of directors for the VA Fisher House
Milwaukee (5 percent of his book's proceeds go to this organization). The Fisher House provides a "home away from
home" for military and veterans' families. In addition, he was
appointed to the CX University Excellence Board and also
serves on their thought leader/teaching facility with some of
the most innovative minds in the CX field.

He learned early on what great customer service looks like when he sold seed packets at the tender age of 6 and his first customer wanted their money back when the seeds didn't grow. He refunded the 10 cents and the following year that customer bought his entire catalog.

Visit Brian online at BrianDennisSpeaker.com

CPSIA information can be obtained
at www.ICGtesting.com
Printed in the USA
FFOW05n2111190916

9 780997 675108